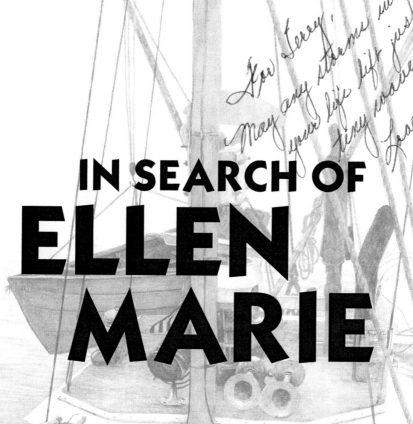

IN SEARCH OF
ELLEN
MARIE

RACHEL ROWLEY SPAULDING

ARCHWAY
PUBLISHING

For Terry —
May any storms in
your life lift just
tiny waves —
Love and hugs
Rachel
9/27/14

Archway Publishing books may be ordered through booksellers or by contacting:

Archway Publishing
1663 Liberty Drive
Bloomington, IN 47403
www.archwaypublishing.com
1-(888)-242-5904

ISBN: 978-1-4808-1044-0 (sc)
ISBN: 978-1-4808-1043-3 (hc)
ISBN: 978-1-4808-1045-7 (e)

Library of Congress Control Number: 2014915168

Printed in the United States of America.

Archway Publishing rev. date: 8/29/2014

Cover painting by artist Arthur Moniz, signature member
of The American Society of Marine Artists

For

Shelly

Contents

Preface

In Search of Ellen Marie came about because I spent two thousand dollars on an original fine-art rendering of the wheelhouse of a commercial fishing vessel even though I wasn't particularly interested in boats or knowledgeable about the fishing industry. Finding the boat became an obsession. Certain friends weren't satisfied with my explanation and kept asking what motivated me. I answered that the pride of owning the original painting of *Ellen Marie* and information gleaned from researching the boatyard where she was built somehow morphed into passionate curiosity. A plethora of coincidences throughout the search settled a veil of mystique over it all. I secretly wondered if an unseen power was driving the quest for its own purposes.

I wrote about the adventure for my own enjoyment until I realized the enormity of its impact on me. I contacted former classmates who lived close to the New Bedford, Massachusetts, fishing port like I did and asked if they were familiar with port activity. An overwhelming majority were not. They wanted to know about my *Ellen Marie* adventure. So I finished writing *In Search of* Ellen Marie to make it possible for everyone to enjoy the sleuthing and to have their hearts touched and minds enlightened by following the path that solved the mystery of *Ellen Marie*'s whereabouts.

I wrote it as well to fulfill a wish of a fisherman who won my heart as he told me about his seventeen years aboard *Ellen Marie*. Captain Arnold "Woodie" Bowers desired for younger generations to know what his fishing experience was like. It is my desire that the book raise curiosity and supportive awareness about the fishing industry and the challenges its people face. I hope that all readers, whether natives, tourists, students, wooden boat enthusiasts, or marine historians, will be entertained by the book's comic stories and enriched by what they learn. May the fishing community find hope that eyes of understanding are opening.

With a soft spot for those who worked or still work on eastern-rig draggers, I offer *In Search of* Ellen Marie as a tribute to all fishermen and to those who have waited, wait now, or will wait for loved ones to return from the sea.

I owe a debt of gratitude to every person named in the book. Each one contributed in positive ways. They know what they did. My heartfelt thanks go to Norman Stone for his encouragement, without which *In Search of* Ellen Marie might not have been completed.

Introduction

In Search of Ellen Marie will take us to Maine's tranquil coastal town South Bristol, home of the prestigious Harvey Gamage Shipyard, where we'll receive a useful phone number from a suntanned fisherman. In New Bedford, Massachusetts, one of the most important fishing ports in the United States, we'll tour the harbor, be emotionally moved by a Harbor Commission employee, and make progress with the help of a nearby multitasking fishing-supply shopkeeper. Captain Woodie Bowers will take the wheel for *Ellen Marie*'s imaginary trip to Georges Bank fishing grounds, share poignant experiences, and explain the fishing process. Captain Alan Cass will take us aboard *Challenge* for a satisfying review of how to fish aboard our boat. We'll experience Boston's North End Fisherman's Feast before returning to South Bristol, where two of *Ellen Marie*'s storytelling boatbuilders may make you laugh. We'll meet another of *Ellen Marie*'s captains at a Newport, Rhode Island, dock. He will tell of drama on stormy winter seas. Soon the mystery of *Ellen Marie*'s location will be solved.

Chapter 1
It Began with Burnt Sienna

It began with burnt sienna. At least I thought it did until artist Arthur Moniz corrected me. No, not burnt sienna but a combination of yellow ochre, cadmium red, and Windsor yellow had captivated me and wouldn't let me go. I kept thinking about that painting. Not the mast, lifeboat, or wheelhouse but the color in the print entitled *The Pilot House* kept tugging at me. Since I knew nothing about fishing boats, it seemed odd that the painting had that kind of power over me. That's what I told John as we devoured scallops and Caesar salad at the Candleworks Restaurant near the working waterfront in New Bedford, Massachusetts.[1] CPA John Hodgson and I had enjoyed a business relationship for years. It had expanded into occasional discussions over lunch after we discovered our mutual spiritual interests. "I'd love for you to see the print," I said after the waiter left the bill.

"Well, let's go," he responded as he put his linen napkin down. "I intended to ask you if you were interested in going for a walk."

---

1   New Bedford, Massachusetts, home of the Whaling National Historical Park, is known as America's number 1 fishing port based on value of fish landings.

John held open the heavy green door as we emerged from the dark restaurant foyer into sunshine. Seagulls squawked above. I smiled, thinking that they always say, "Welcome to New Bedford." We climbed four granite steps, turned left onto Water Street, crossed cobblestones to the other side, and turned right onto William Street. We walked beyond the Whaling Museum to the Arthur Moniz Gallery in the building sided with yellow clapboard.

A tinkling bell announced us. Soft music invited us to relax and peruse Mr. Moniz's magnificent, highly detailed graphite and watercolor renderings—boats of New Bedford's fishing industry, local scenes of life both wild and still. "That's the one," I whispered as I pointed to the print that leaned against a display box on the floor. It was mounted, not framed. John seemed genuinely interested in my attraction to the painting and saw its beauty—that shade of orange that contrasted with the white wheelhouse; the gray blues of the pilot house roof; and the fog-enshrouded, mildly rolling sea with its additional hint of green. I'm ashamed to admit that the child in me wished that he would buy the print for me like my father would have.

Weeks passed before I acted on my desire to have that special print. As I drove south along Route 195 from my hometown, Wareham, to New Bedford, hope battled a nagging fear that I might have to bear consequences for my procrastination. When I didn't see either the special print or the display box that it had leaned against, I described to the gallery employee what I was seeking. "That's gone," she said. "I sold it a couple weeks ago."

"Oh," I sighed, letting my shoulders droop. *Oh, well,* I thought. *I've lived with faded wallpaper and second-hand furniture for a long time. I guess I'll do it a while longer.* I wanted *The Pilot House* to inspire a new color scheme, to bid dingy décor good-bye.

But my desire didn't die. There were other giclée[2] prints of *The Pilot House*—traditionally framed or matted ones that I could have purchased. Should I have bought one of those? *There's the graphite and watercolor original,* I thought. Its larger size convinced me to return to the gallery for another look.

Once again, the bell tinkled its welcome, and I wandered past paintings of whaling vessels, lighthouses, fishing boats, scallop shells, and a

---

2   inkjet produced

*We walked along the New Bedford cobblestone streets
past the Whaling Museum to the Moniz Gallery.*

poster of Oak Bluffs. Intrigued by the lack of color in one painting, I
stopped to appreciate the lone detailed blue and black mussel against a
stark background of black and white stones before sauntering to the rear
west wall where the original of *The Pilot House* hung. It wasn't as large as
I remembered. I stood there mulling over arguments for and against my
potential purchase. *It's a lot of money for me. Am I insane?* The battle waged
until I purchased an unframed giclée print. Cheryl Moniz, Arthur's wife,
was working in the gallery that day. I told her my plan to redecorate my
living room around *The Pilot House.*

"Will you be getting new furniture and everything?" she asked.

"Everything," I affirmed.

"I'll put chips of colors that would work on a card for you. It will
help you with your choices."

She was right. That card and the print itself inspired decorating
purchases that spanned February, March, and April 2006. Flooring had
to be installed, furniture made, area rugs fabricated, and painting done.
Construction and waiting for deliveries threatened to push the project

into July. And something bothered me. The giclée print in its simple white mat looked lost against the living-room wall.

On July 7, 2006, I returned to the gallery, took a leap of faith, and bought the original painting. Cheryl took frame samples from the wall behind the counter and placed them against the painting.

"I like that one," I said, pointing to a blue-toned rough wood frame with an inner edge that looked like blue and gold rope.

"These are the mats that would work," she said, laying four against the inside of the frame. One accentuated the rust colors of the winch and deck; another brought out the blue of the pilot house roof. I chose a sand color for an inside mat and plain white for the main mat; the pale colors would beautifully contrast with the dark gray-blue wall where I planned to hang the painting.

On July 15, everything in the living room coordinated with *The Pilot House,* from the Japanese cherry flooring to the sand-color couches, the terra cotta–color chair and ottoman, and the gray-blue walls and white trim. I hung the painting with immense satisfaction.

Cheryl had said that Arthur would give me the identity and history of the boat, but when I picked up the painting, no information accompanied it. The clerk behind the counter didn't know about Cheryl's promise. I had looked forward to learning something about the boat, especially her name. I hoped they wouldn't let me down.

Chapter 2
The Internet Ride

I thumbed through the mail before closing my Mansfield post office box. Tucked between the Visa bill and the Chico's ad was a small envelope bearing the return address of the Moniz Gallery. Arthur Moniz had not let me down. Delighted, I rushed to the parking lot; in my idling car, I carefully ripped open Arthur's envelope. A notecard depicted *Morning Mist*—his painting of a small boat, blue below the water line, perfectly reflected, floating close to the grassy marsh shore. Inside the card, Arthur had artfully printed, "The painting that you recently purchased, *The Pilot House,* is of an old New Bedford dragger named *Ellen Marie.* She was built in South Bristol, Maine, in 1962 at Harvey Gamage's. The captain was a man from Nova Scotia named Woodie Bowers. I had an old photo from about 1968 that was the idea for the painting."

I wondered where South Bristol was, thinking that it might be nice to get away for a while. Between work and my mother's health issues, I was close to burning out. My tan Corolla maneuvered the dip out of the post office lot, turned left, and then right onto Copeland.

Benny, my overweight tiger cat, welcomed me home, purring loudly and rubbing his head and belly against my legs. I added the mail to the pile on the counter. Benny gobbled his Fancy Feast chicken hearts;

the microwave buzzed its eight-minute countdown toward hot mixed vegetables.

The old Windows 98 booted up faster than the up-to-date computer at work would have. I studied MapQuest's suggested route from Massachusetts to South Bristol on the coastal map. The blue line wiggled through familiar places like Portland, Brunswick, Bath, and Wiscasset. Zooming in to clarify a hairpin turn, I saw Damariscotta at the top of the arch. I remembered wishing twenty years before that I could take time to explore Damariscotta, but I had passed its exit, continuing to Rockland to catch the Vinalhaven ferry. The new opportunity pleased me.

The South Bristol website grabbed my interest like a good book captures a voracious reader. The small fishing town, described as a resort with "only 897 inhabitants in 2000," boasted three nature preserves and a history of making bricks. The area had supplied bricks for buildings in Boston's Back Bay. I pictured that neighborhood's familiar three-story edifices. A general mention of shipbuilding—schooners, fishing trawlers, lobster boats, and yachts—must have referred to Harvey Gamage's.

I took note of two bed and breakfasts in South Bristol for future reference. Without giving dinner a second thought, I typed "Harvey Gamage Shipyard" and hit the search icon.

The first linked website opened with an image of jagged icy mountain peaks, frigid-looking water, and a man in the forefront dressed in a fur-lined parka—the polar opposite of my idea of an August minivacation on the coast of Maine. I shuddered with the thought of the cold. "One of the local places," I read, "is Gamage Point." That surprised me, because I didn't realize there was civilization in the Antarctic. Gamage Point, I learned, was named after the Harvey Gamage Shipyard because Harvey Gamage built the Antarctic research vessel *Hero*.

Once, years earlier, I had sailed on a marine research vessel—the barkentine *Regina Maris*. In the early 1980s, my Suffolk University marine biology class with Ocean Research and Education Society members sailed from Puerto Rico to St. John to research coral. I always wore a bathing suit and never a pair of shoes. That's my style: no parkas and no ice for me.

I exited the Antarctic website and clicked the next link, where I read about sailing on the ninety-five-foot *Mary Day* in Maine's Penobscot

Bay.[3] The only thing gentler than the windjammer's six-knot speed, I imagined, was the perfect warm summer breeze. The link was the door to Michael Fralich's written experience aboard this schooner, which was built in 1962—the same year, reportedly, as *Ellen Marie*—at the Harvey Gamage Shipyard.

The next link introduced me to Roswell C. Ellinwood by way of his obituary in the *Boothbay Register*. Mr. Ellinwood had supplied timber to the Harvey Gamage Shipyard—maybe wood from which *Ellen Marie* had been built.

I moved on to a *Fisherman's Voice* article about a Mr. Kass who had worked at the Harvey Gamage Shipyard. The article characterized the Gamage Yard as "Ivy League."[4] To me, that meant that *Ellen Marie* was, to use a cliché, the top of the line. She became even more precious after that.

The reference to Mr. Kass building wood lobster boats triggered memories of my visit to Vinalhaven. In the '70s, home was a condominium in Brookline near Cleveland Circle and Boston College. The caretakers, Bob and Dottie Foote, and I became friends. Dottie was raised on Vinalhaven. Several times I rejected invitations to vacation with them on the island until Dottie told me that she had been out on a lobster boat that belonged to her brother-in-law, Junior. I accompanied her and Bob on the next trip.

The island was quiet at 3:00 a.m. when Dottie and I, half asleep, bounced down the hill in Junior's truck. Bob preferred sleeping to fishing. Junior gave us a hand getting into the double-ender at the dock. Steve, Junior's deckhand with shoulder-length blond hair and a bucket cap, rowed us to the lobster boat. I can see its red hull and green wheelhouse in my mind now as clearly as if I were actually looking at it anchored in Vinalhaven Harbor. By daylight, we had arrived at Junior's strings of lobster pots, but ocean swells and lack of horizon had made me violently ill. A bench that would have made a good bunk if it had had a mattress hugged the curve of the bow. I lay down on it with my head

---

3   Michael Fralic, "Greetings From Norubega," *The Gray News* 34, no. 22 (May 31, 2002):1

4   Mike Crow, "You Have To Love This Work," *Fishermen's Voice* 9, no. 8 (August 2004) http://www.fishermensvoice.com/archives/august 04.html

on a coil of rope and fell sound asleep as if the revving diesel engine was playing lullabies. When I woke feeling perfectly well, the sun was shining. Junior, wearing orange bib overalls and a yellow sou'wester to keep the sun from burning the top of his head, ran the winch to haul traps to the surface. Steve, also in orange bibs, lifted traps into the boat. Flocks of seagulls squawked, impatiently waiting for Steve to empty the old bait remains into the ocean. I refilled the bait bags with slippery herring and gave them to Steve to tie into the traps that would go back to the sea. After Junior taught me how to hold them without getting hurt, I banded the lobsters. I stretched elastic bands with a scissor-like tool designed for the purpose and slipped the elastic over the claws. Dottie, who had been sleeping down forward for most of the trip, reappeared when we cruised into the harbor. After the catch was unloaded and weighed, Junior gave her lobsters, which she boiled for our dinner. For a long time after, I wouldn't pay restaurant prices for lobster.

When I read about *Candy B II* in the next link of the shipyard search, my high spirits plummeted.[5] Harvey Gamage had built the scalloper in 1950. In 2003, she had sunk fifty miles southeast of Nantucket. Four fishermen had lost their lives. Two booms had been added to her, making her top-heavy, the year before. It was difficult for me to believe that such a tragedy had befallen a Gamage boat, and I reasoned that the Harvey Gamage Yard couldn't have added the booms. Suddenly I remembered Raymie.

More than twenty years before, a Boston fishing-boat captain named Raymond Bono had agreed to take my camera and me on a fishing trip to Georges Bank, but because of insurance issues, he had changed his mind and said I couldn't go. On his next trip, the one I had hoped to take, the boat took on water. I think it was the *St. Jude*. There was a dramatic Coast Guard rescue of all the crew, but the boat sank.

The next computer link took me back to New Bedford, where I had purchased my painting of *Ellen Marie*. *Standard Times* staff writer Jack Stewardson had written about a 1961 Gamage dragger, the *Angela W*, going back to sea one last time. I stared at her picture.

---

5   Steve Cartwright, "Coast Guard: scalloper lost at sea was over-rigged," *Fishing* (March 2005): 1

She looked much like *Ellen Marie*. But bereft of her rigging, her paint faded and scraped, *Angela W* was no more than an empty hull robbed of purpose. Arthur Moniz had painted *Ellen Marie* to look young, vibrant, and ready to work.

The article said that *Angela W* had retired under the federal government's fishing vessel buyback effort. Her family had decided that it would be a dignified end to have *Angela W* scuttled off Cox's Ledge, about thirty miles south of New Bedford. The reporter explained that the federal government had designed a program to reduce the number of fishing boats in an attempt to preserve codfish, haddock, and yellowtail flounder, species whose populations were threatened by overfishing. More than seventy vessels had been taken. Boat owners had to surrender their fishing permits and destroy or change the use of their vessels.

Angela W's owners decided to give her a dignified end. Isn't that what we do to hopeless pets? To me, the federal government taking those fishing vessels was like euthanizing seventy beloved pets. I imagined the emotional pain that boat owners must have experienced. What about the economic impact on the city of New Bedford? Was that considered?

I continued to read, afraid of what I might find. Had *Ellen Marie* been one of the seventy? Had she been scrapped, scuttled, or used for something else?

Mr. Stewardson, wrote in the *Standard Times*, "Most of those sold in New Bedford have been ripped apart for scrap, but the *Angela W* was an old wooden dragger with little scrap value, so the owners sought permission from the Coast Guard and the Environmental Protection Agency to sink it 30 miles out to sea in about 140 feet of water."[6]

From the Ivy League to "little scrap value"—what a contrast! *Angela W* and Mr. Stewardson led me to wonder with apprehension about *Ellen Marie's* fate. His newspaper article ended with a list of the retired New Bedford boats. I felt as if I was about to read a tragic list like a report of soldiers killed in action. She wasn't there.

There were more links to other websites in my Harvey Gamage Shipyard search, but sadness had sapped my enthusiasm. I didn't really

6   Jack Stewardson, "Boat's end is 'a fitting tribute' to its career at sea," *Standard Times, South Coast Today* (January 21, 1998)

want to go on, but I clicked other links anyway—the website of the *Appledore,* the last schooner custom built by the Harvey Gamage Shipyard in 1978, and an uplifting *Boothbay Register* article entitled "Bringing New Life to a Maine Classic." Daniel Fayen wrote about a boatbuilder, Tony Finocchiaro, who was restoring a 1977 Gamage Shipyard lobster boat. [7]

Hooray for restoration!

What a ride I had taken on the waves of data transmission—from the icy Antarctic to a summer windjammer cruise off the coast of Maine, from a timber supplier to one lobster boatbuilder and another restorer, from the Ivy League to mere emotional value, from loss of human life to preservation of fish life!

Ellen Marie, *You weren't taken by the government. Where are you? I have to know!*

I impulsively sent off an e-mail to my friends Charlie and Elaine Coupe, who were building a house in Northport, Maine, asking if they'd like to rendezvous if I went to South Bristol.

"Let us know when you're coming down," Charlie responded as if he were a native. An outsider would have said "coming *up.* "

Sometimes I say I'm interested in a course of action but don't follow through. It wasn't going to happen this time.

I chose to drive to South Bristol the week after Labor Day so that traffic would be less of a hassle and made a reservation at the Unique Yankee B&B. Exhaling slowly, I sat back satisfied, locked my fingers behind my gray-haired head, and wondered what I'd learn about *Ellen Marie* in her birthplace.

---

7   Daniel Fayen, "Bringing New Life To A Maine Classic," *Boothbay Register* 127, no. 34 (Aug 19, 2004)

Chapter 3
The Harbor Tour

In mid-August, when my life-long friend Marie called from New Hampshire requesting an overnight stay with me, I welcomed her visit. A day off would be refreshing. I began to think of what we could do together.

A few days later, I called to tell her about an activity that I hoped she'd favor because it would give me a chance to look for *Ellen Marie*. "I saw an ad in the *Wanderer* for a New Bedford harbor tour," I said. "What do you think?"

"Oh," she said. "That sounds like fun."

The sun blessed us everywhere we went on August 23. We parked in the Candleworks Restaurant lot and walked across the footbridge to the other side of Route 18. The footbridge steps emptied out in front of the north door of the New Bedford Visitors Center—a small brick building at the beginning of the fish pier. We saw the small tour boat with a blue canopy tied up next to the south side of the visitors center. Tourists comfortably milled in and around the center in anticipation of the captain's arrival. We were twenty minutes early, so Marie and I perused the exhibit inside. Beneath one of the windows were two hinged blue blocks of wood, each topped with a polished steel silhouette of a fishing vessel. I lifted the one that looked most like *Ellen Marie*, with the pilot house in the stern, a style identified as an eastern-rig dragger as opposed to a western-rig dragger that had the pilot house up front. These were new terms to me.

A blackboard resembling the records of a fish auction covered an entire wall. I read the name of each boat and the list of fish it had brought in until I saw *Ellen Marie*. I wanted to scream, "Marie! Come see!" Instead, I weaved through pillars of people, grabbed my friend by the arm, and insisted in a polite tone of voice, "Come here! I have to show you something." There it was: *Ellen Marie* written in white chalk with a list of her catch—haddock, cod, flounder, lemon sole, the number of pounds of each and the price. Her column on the blackboard was behind and immediately to the right of a portrait on see-through screening of the head and shoulders of a pipe-smoking man—a fisherman, I assumed.

Of course, Marie did not share my level of excitement. Neither did the National Park Ranger when I asked her, "What can you tell me about the boats listed on the blackboard?"

"Nothing," she said. "That's just a display set up to look like an auction from years ago."

"But the boat *Ellen Marie* is real," I insisted. "I have her picture. I'm trying to find her."

"I don't know anything about her," she repeated, looking down at the counter. "You could try the Harbor Commission. It's just over there," she said, pointing toward the other side of the pier. "Two buildings beyond the footbridge."

I would have visited the Harbor Commission, but it was time to board the small tour boat. The captain, dressed in khaki pants, a white shirt, and a white bucket hat, stood dockside collecting tickets as we filed down a shallow ramp to the boat. When he embarked I asked, "Would it be all right if I sit here?" I pointed to the top of the engine compartment, a seat-height box up forward and center.

"Sure," the captain said. "It's the best seat there is."

I motioned for Marie to join me, but she sat opposite me on the bench that skirted the perimeter of the boat. The captain steered away from the pier and headed south. We passed fishing vessels tied at the docks bow-to-stern like an elephant parade and three deep. I searched for *Ellen Marie*, but it was impossible to read all the names. I told the captain about my quest.

"Not familiar with an *Ellen Marie*," he said.

"It's an eastern-rig dragger," I informed him, trying to be smart with what I had learned from the identified silhouettes in the visitors center.

"I don't think there are many wooden draggers around anymore." He grabbed his microphone to address everyone. "This is the Acushnet River," he said. "It's the largest river that flows into Buzzards Bay." He informed us that New Bedford was the top fishing port in the country based on the value of the catch—mostly scallops. What we were headed for was the marine structure of New Bedford's hurricane barrier. He explained that the tower controlled hydraulically operated doors that, when closed, shut out the surge of seawater that might accompany a bad storm like a hurricane. "The barrier includes the twenty-foot-high stone riprap you've driven by," he said, "if you've been out to Rodman Point or Davey's Locker restaurant."

We cruised out to open water before reversing direction to view the Fairhaven waterfront opposite the New Bedford docks. The captain pointed to a black boat in dry dock. "That's the *Ernestina*, a schooner that was built in 1894 for the Gloucester fishing fleet." He said she might be on display at one of the New Bedford piers in September.

I leaned from my engine compartment seat toward Marie next to me on the bench. "Having fun?"

"I'm having a ball!" She eased some of her blowing blond hair away from her lips and snapped a photo of the *Ernestina*.

I shivered in the cool shadow of Fairhaven Bridge. The captain pointed out that the span connected the New Bedford mainland to two islands and to Fairhaven. He explained that the swing bridge opened hourly over the gap between Fish Island and Pope's Island to allow bigger boats to enter the inner harbor.

I saw no boats named *Ellen Marie* in the inner harbor. As we floated under the swing bridge on the return trip, I looked up to the eerie green grating. The captain said that the harbor was full of 329 whaling ships in 1857 and we could board a half-scale replica of one at the Whaling Museum. He eased his boat along the dock and secured it by wrapping ropes fore and aft around stanchions.

"Thanks! Nice tour," I said to him when our eyes met. He smiled.

Walking through the Visitors Center, I glanced over to *Ellen Marie* written on the blackboard. I hoped the Harbor Commission office would help me find her.

Marie and I walked to the Harbor Commission reception desk, where a young woman looked up from her work. I asked her if she could help me locate a boat.

"I might be able to," she said, swiveling to face her computer. "What's her name?"

"*Ellen Marie.*"

Everything about the receptionist expressed desire to help—her smile, her bright tone of voice, and the way she sat leaning forward with eye contact before she turned. I relaxed as she typed, waited, entered something more, and waited a few more seconds.

"Eight vessels are coming up with that name."

It hadn't occurred to me that there might be multiple boats with the same name. She turned the computer screen so we both could read it. I commented as we scrolled through the information, "That recreational vessel wouldn't be her. It's way too old—1926. Mine was built in the '60s ... A towing vessel in Iowa? I doubt it ... No, that one's too new. ... Ah. A commercial fishing vessel. That's what mine is, but the one that's showing up was built in 1977 ... Wait. There's one built in 1968. Could the date be wrong? But it's fishing in Washington. That doesn't seem likely. My *Ellen Marie* fished out of New Bedford."

The build dates for the remaining boats spanned 1983 to 2001—too new to be my *Ellen Marie.*

"Every boat has a documentation number," the young woman explained. "It stays the same—with the boat. If you get more information, I could search again."

"Thanks so much for trying," I said, determined to obtain more information somehow.

"Any time," she said.

Marie had been entertaining herself by reading posters and pamphlets. She put one down as I approached her. "No luck," I said. Chances of finding a documentation number seemed remote since a Harbor Commission employee couldn't even find her name. I hid my disappointment and focused on giving Marie the attention she deserved. But inside I was like a racehorse behind the starting gate. I wanted to get back on the computer to search for *Ellen Marie.*

Chapter 4
The Dragger

The day after the New Bedford harbor tour, I booted up the computer to look for my boat. Twelve seconds of electronic processing seemed like enough time to read *War and Peace*. The search for *Ellen Marie* generated twenty-four million hits. Realizing that I had included anything and anybody named Ellen Marie, I added *dragger* to the search to narrow the results. I read a site description and, not trusting my comprehension, jerked forward in my chair and read it again.

I clicked the mouse and began to scan the full article about boats until I found the intriguing phrase: "… skipper of the Gamage built 80 ft. Fishing Vessel *Ellen Marie* is quoted in his book 'The Dragger' by William Finn …"

There's a book written about her! Focusing intently on the keyboard, I punched keys until "The Dragger" and "William Finn" appeared in the search line and poked Enter.

Three resultant websites advertised the book for sale and listed phone numbers. I picked up the handset to my old white phone, grabbing the base before the coiled cord pulled it off the desk. I punched in the first phone number and listened to the ringing. No answer. It was after five. Maybe this was an office number. Neither the second nor third seller answered either, which I thought was strange. Undaunted, I searched again and found other sites that were selling copies of *The Dragger*. One advertised an autographed book and included an e-mail address. I inquired about the book's availability and price. His response arrived the same day:

> Yes, the book is available for $20 plus $3.50 shipping. It is autographed, first edition with a dust jacket. There is one small tear in the dust jacket on the back. The book is in otherwise fine condition, in my opinion.
>
> Alden

"Belfast, Maine," appeared under his name. I wondered if Belfast was close enough to save time and money with an in-person purchase.

I pulled up the area map on MapQuest. Belfast, Maine was too far north—adjacent to Northport, where I had a planned rendezvous with Charlie and Elaine in fourteen days. Of all the books that were available, what were the chances of me finding and choosing one so close to my Maine destination?

I contacted the bookseller again, telling him of my plan to be in the area on September 7 and asking if I could pick up the book in person. That was fine with Alden, and I was Yankee-minded enough to save the shipping cost. He gave me his address—Harbor Hill just off Route 1.

"This is getting interesting," I wrote to Charlie and Elaine. "I now have an errand close to you: I'm picking up a book, *The Dragger*, I found on the Internet from a man who lives at Harbor Hill in Belfast. This is all happening because I was drawn to the color orange. I'll explain when I see you."

Charlie confirmed that Harbor Hill was about six miles from them, just over the bridge. He suggested that I arrive before lunch and stay for the night.

One evening on a whim, I stopped at the Mansfield Library to see if *The Dragger* was in the system. There were two copies—one in Taunton and one in Middleboro.

If patience is a virtue, then I admit to being driven by vice to see

The Dragger as soon as possible. It didn't matter that within two weeks' time I would have my own copy. The following Thursday, August 31, I drove ten minutes from my Rochester office to the Middleboro Library. After parking in the dirt lot across Peirce Street, I marched through the double doors and upstairs to one of the computer cubicles to the right of the crescent-shaped circulation desk. Once I found the call number, I grabbed a stubby yellow pencil and a scrap of paper from the purple plastic basket and wrote, "639.22." On my way to the stacks, I passed a computer that blipped each time the librarian held a book under a purple light. Number ranges on the ends of the gunmetal bookshelves led me to the stack directly behind the desk. Black, rectangular signs stuck out every two or three feet perpendicular to the top of the shelves: Pets, Gardening, Automotive, Pregnancy. Down the line, eye-level numbers on book spines descended well below that of *The Dragger*. I had to backtrack and stoop down to a low shelf under Pets. With my index finger on the top of its spine, I eased 639.22 out of its niche between *Whaling Wives* and *Leviathan*. *The Dragger* was without a jacket, gray and faded as if it had lain under another book in the sun.

The library's hanging light fixtures, shaped like half globes, cast a calming green apple haze on the walls. I took my prize to a blue, boxy armchair. A woman in a purple sweater sat across from me absorbed in a magazine, her black-stockinged foot resting against the low glass table between us.

After settling into the chair, I eagerly opened *The Dragger* as if raising the lid on a pirate's treasure chest. It had been published in 1970. The front endpapers consisted of a chart labeled "Georges Bank and Nantucket Shoals"—a chart that "bears Captain Bowers' markings of wrecks (including rock outcroppings) that might cause damage or loss to *Ellen Marie*'s nets." In the acknowledgments, author William Finn explained that *Ellen Marie*'s owner, Rudolph Matland, gave him permission to take his camera on a fishing trip to Georges Bank—much like I had wanted to do with Raymond Bono in the 1980s. Having seen the pictures, one of Finn's friends suggested that they would make a good book. Finn wrote that his work was accomplished under conditions of ignorance, seasickness, and fear. I was sure that my conditions, especially ignorance and fear, would have been worse than his if I had gone to Georges Bank with Raymie.

I turned the page. One full page could not contain all of *Ellen Marie*'s pilot house, mast, and lifeboat—so recognizable even in black and white. There was one big difference between the photo in the book and my painting of *Ellen Marie*. In the photo, a smiling man peering from the wheelhouse held his elbow outside the lowered starboard window. His presence seemed to bring her to life!

Page after page, Finn's written experience and photography helped me to bond with my *Ellen Marie*, her body, soul, and purpose. I read about her captain and crew, saw her photographed gunnels leaning into a stormy sea, and learned at least something about her fishing process. Her net went over the side, not the stern. She was known as a *high-liner*. I didn't completely understand the term, but because she was a high-liner, Captain Bowers had been able to take on the strongest, most experienced crew members. *Ellen Marie* came from the Ivy League of boatyards. Now I knew she had had the best crew.

I was tired by the time I reached the end of the book, where I scanned a marine architect's drawings and looked at net designs in the appendix. I had reviewed the book thoroughly so that I no longer felt overly anxious to have my trophy copy. I could wait the seven days.

I returned *The Dragger* to its slot between *Whaling Wives* and *Leviathan* and floated out of the library richer with education, looking forward to adventure in Maine.

Very visuAL, RAchael
ImAginat,on
Wonderful.

Chapter 5
The Buyback Program

It was just a feeling, like a sixth sense, that learning more about the buyback program might give me a clue to *Ellen Marie*'s whereabouts. I hoped that a word, a name, a detail of some sort would be the key to unlock the mystery. So I went on a fishing expedition of my own—a relentless Internet search to net the government agency responsible for the buyback. The search hauled in the website of the Office of Sustainable Development and Intergovernmental Affairs—an office within National Oceanic and Atmospheric Administration (NOAA) in the Department of Commerce. There was a summary of the Program on the site. More than surprised, I was embarrassed when I read that the Fishing Capacity Reduction Demonstration Program (FCRDP) was described as a "voluntary program." I'd thought that it had been forced on fishermen, analogous to tearing beloved pets out of owners' arms.

The program had targeted full-time groundfish vessels. Since *Ellen Marie* was a groundfish dragger, she qualified. Applicants had been required to submit financial information that NOAA personnel had plugged into a formula for scoring and ranking. The government paid

1.89 million dollars for eleven fishing vessels. Everything of salvageable value, mostly metal, was stripped off the boats, and the boats, like *Angela W*, were sunk. Associated fishing permits were turned over. When *was* her dignified demise? Since participation in the program had been voluntary, I supposed *Ellen Marie's* owner simply could have chosen not to submit a bid and keep her fishing. It was also possible that she hadn't been chosen after her financial information had been scored and ranked through the NOAA formula. But neither of those possibilities explained why she didn't appear on the Harbor Commission computer screen.

Searching for the government agency and reviewing the FCRDP seemed like it had been a waste of time, yet that strange sixth sense was telling me that I was getting closer to the goal. How, I didn't know. And why was there an undulating dark cloud inside me?

I took off my glasses, put them on the desk, and rubbed my eyes. In the morning, I would be leaving for South Bristol. Certainly I would learn something there that would lead me to *Ellen Marie*.

Chapter 6
On the Way to South Bristol

If the Toyota had been a convertible, I might have dared to take both hands off the wheel, thrust my fists up in the air and yell, "I'm free!" Instead, I slipped a book on CD, *One for the Money* by Janet Evanovich, into the slot in the dashboard and listened to the female reader say, "There are some men who enter a woman's life and screw it up forever."

"Hah!" I said. "How well I know." It sounded like I wouldn't be bored on the four-hour drive to South Bristol, Maine.

About half past noon, more than two hours into the trip, I turned the car off the highway into the Kennebunk rest area and parked close to a picnic grove. Sitting at the red table where I ate my prepacked lunch was like having a front-row circus seat. Two Weimaraners and a greyhound pranced in the fenced dog-walking area to my left as if they were being judged at a prestigious kennel club show. In front of me, a stick of a man led his white miniature poodle back and forth on the sidewalk, patrolling the parking lot. He repeatedly tugged on the leash, lifting the poor little pup right off the ground. Closer to Burger King, a man and a woman stood beside their black Bronco, each taking turns pinching a portion of food from their plates, reaching through the open window and feeding their spaniel, who sat in the front passenger's seat.

A tractor-trailer truck's engine revved. The truck lurched and slightly separated from its trailer before the driver cut the engine. Another rig, a twin of the other—silver with green, soft, tied-down sides—backed in parallel to the first. Were they going to switch trailers? As I watched in wonder, I thought of the Simon and Garfunkel song "America," in which two friends on a bus are "playing games with the faces." "She said, 'The man in the gabardine suit is a spy.' I said, 'Be careful, his bow tie is really a camera.'" I wondered what Paul Simon might imagine for the truck intrigue and laughed at myself for being easily amused. I snapped the lid onto my Tupperware container and walked to the car. My curiosity about the trailer trucks evaporated like a dissipating morning fog as I accelerated along I-95, praising the contrast of white birches against dark browns and greens in the roadside forest. The shades of green seemed countless against the consistently blue sky. I pressed play to resume amusement from bounty hunter Stephanie Plum's antics in *One for the Money*.

It had been more than twenty years since I traveled the coastal route during the days when Bob and Dotty Foote and I visited her relatives on Vinalhaven. In Wiscasset, I looked for Tat's Diner, but another restaurant had taken its place, and the two schooners that used to be an attraction in the harbor had deteriorated to nonexistence.

Damariscotta, with its Rexall Drug Store, bookshop, and café, would have been a good backdrop for Norman Rockwell's painting of a family on an outing in their Woodie station wagon.

I turned right off Main Street, just beyond the drug store, onto Bristol Road, Route 129. South Bristol was less than a half-hour ahead. My excitement manifested in a noticeably strong heartbeat. As I descended a hill, the town loomed before me, and a sign for Gamage Shipyard made me want to turn right, but I couldn't. My need for a pit stop compelled me to press on toward the B&B.

Chapter 7
South Bristol

Gravel crunched under my Toyota's tires as I drove up the hill to the Unique Yankee Bed and Breakfast. The driveway curved to the rear of the modern house that boasted a fenced wrap-around deck and a tower for viewing sections of South Bristol, inlets, and the Atlantic beyond. Inside, light from the huge, oak-trimmed windows and skylights in the cathedral ceiling enhanced pristine white walls and an open two-story floor plan. An oblong cherry dining table with glass inserts and chairs upholstered in a blue and mauve pattern paralleled the window wall. Seascapes, lighthouses, shells, a ship model, and a world globe decorated the interior. Proprietor Cheryl Munson, a lovely, soft-spoken woman, welcomed me and led me past the living room's white sofas to my room.

It had everything—TV, DVD player, refrigerator, and microwave. A white rattan chair and floor lamp provided a great place to read, and the glass-topped bamboo table and two cushioned chairs offered a place for lunch. Sliders opened to my own private corner of the deck. I put a few things in the dark patterned French chest of drawers, but I didn't stay long. Gamage pulled me like a magnet.

I decided to walk. The steep gravel driveway emptied onto Coveside Road, a paved way where minutes passed between vehicles. Hemlocks, pines, and oaks towered over me. The fragrances of damp, woodsy earth and salty seaside mud and the silence except for an occasional singing bird and the sound of my sneakers on the pavement were intoxicating. The sweetest breeze, like fine silk, ever so lightly drifted across my face. I passed the white Union Congregational Church with its steeple pointing to the heavens and its red banner proclaiming, "God is still speaking." Farther along, down a side street, I noticed a gray-shingled building—the post office. The noise level was rising. The road descended, curved, and descended again. I could feel the strain in my legs. I turned; the hill looked steep. *I'm going to have to walk up*, I thought. Deciding that the challenge was worth the effort, I continued my trek.

A heavy-set man in a floppy gray hat and a short woman walking close by his side trudged up the hill toward me. With a Scottish brogue, he asked, "Can you tell me, is the post box up this way?"

"Yes, it is," I answered, "on the right. You'll see it down a side street." The fact that I had just arrived yet could help with directions amused me.

A gray, warehouse-size building with a flat roof and two large bay doors—one faded robin's-egg blue, the other weathered natural wood— faced the water on the other side of the harbor. *That must be it*, I thought. Three tiers of windows hung on the length of the rundown building. Many of them were broken; some were boarded up, yet I was anxious to document the place on film. I walked along the side of Maggie's Sea Food to the rear, thinking that the view of the shed where *Ellen Marie* had been built would be unobstructed, but a large tree stood in my way. A seagull squawked. "Don't you laugh at *me*," I kidded, looking up.

Down the road, bells rang, red lights flashed, and red-and-white striped wooden barriers pivoted from vertical to horizontal to stop traffic from crossing the bridge. I followed three boys on bicycles around the barrier and stood in a sandy patch. The green-grated bridge swung horizontally to the east, creating a gap through which the lobster boat *Eliza B* passed to the other side. When the bridge closed, the boys pedaled across. Having made eye contact with the bridge operator, I pointed to myself, then to the sidewalk on the bridge, and raised my shoulders and upturned palms. He nodded, indicating that I had permission to walk across while cars still waited for the barriers to rise. I found a place on the other side of the bridge to photograph the dilapidated big gray building. Jutting out beyond the building at the end of a long wharf was another, more modern building with a red roof. Its sign read Gamage Shipyard.

On the other side of the road, Osier's store window advertised crab-meat, lobsters, and groceries. A man pumped gasoline into his old green pickup truck sandwiched between the road and storefront. Fishing boats waited at the dock next door. Mud glistened below black stained rocks at the edge of the eelgrass. The sounds of hammering and of boards dropping echoed from the rim of the inner harbor. A short way up the incline, I turned left onto Shipyard Road, admiring Queen Anne's lace and orange lilies in the tall grass along the roadside. A car door slammed. A man carried luggage toward a stately white house, beyond which was posted a green sign that said Gamage Shipyard Office & Entrance.

A gravel yard led to the rear of the big gray building with broken windows. I peeked through an ajar door expecting to see a cavernous interior but instead discovered a small bathroom in surprisingly good condition. My trek continued around the right side of the building down to the end of the wharf. The door to the building with the red roof was open wide, inviting entrance to a bright room with a sales counter, light-colored shelving with a sparse collection of boat-related goods for sale, and no one around to sell them.

"Hello?" I called.

"Be right down," a man's voice answered.

A moment later, I introduced myself.

"Hi. I'm Steve," he said. "What can I do for ya?"

"I bought a painting of the groundfish dragger *Ellen Marie*," I explained. "When the artist told me that the boat was built in South Bristol at the Harvey Gamage Shipyard, I wanted to see the yard and learn what I could about *Ellen Marie*."

"Look in there," he suggested, pointing to a white three-ring binder on the counter. "It's a collection that Larry put together of photos of boats built at the Harvey Gamage Yard."

While I flipped through the pages of photo-bearing acetate sleeves, he said, "The big shed was erected in the 1940s. Before that, boats were built outside. Harvey Gamage built boats for the military from 1940 to 1944."

"Oh, here's the *Hero*," I said, excited to see the Antarctic research vessel. "And here's *Angela W*." I told Steve about my Internet search, especially what I learned about *Angela W* and the government buyback program.

"Fishing in South Bristol is about nonexistent now," he volunteered. He explained that the government regulations had cut fishing days for the year down to only forty-eight.

"Forty-eight out of three hundred sixty-five? That's astounding."

Steve apologized for not being more helpful and said that I should talk to Larry, who was "around when they were building." He wasn't sure when Larry would be in.

I paid for a blue Gamage Shipyard t-shirt, tucked the top of it into the waistband of my jeans so I didn't have to carry it, expressed my thanks, and left. The door that had been open closed behind me.

A walkway along the north side of Osier's Wharf would lead me to boats docked to the east. Did I have the courage to trespass? I took the risk. I followed the sound of rushing water to the rear of the store, where water flowed into a tank for live lobsters. A man wearing a NASCAR t-shirt and tan shorts walked through the back door carrying a glass-bottled beer. "Got time for a chat?" I asked him.

I told him what Steve had said about limited fishing days. He agreed, adding, "The only way they can make it is if they own more than one boat." He also told me that ship builders from Boothbay had bought the Gamage Yard and that the old shed would be torn down to make way for a new one where upscale yachts would be built.

Gamage Shipyard seemed to be nothing more than an insignificant marina. How had it fallen from the crème de la crème of boatbuilding to this? I wished I could have seen the shed in good condition, alive with a staff of artisans skillfully using tools to craft top-of-the-line wooden vessels.

Part way across the bridge, the bells rang and the red lights flashed,

so I quickened my pace. "You can stay on if you want," the bridge operator said in a Maine drawl, so I rode the bridge as it swung east to let a
lobster boat through.

"Was ya scared?" he asked me after the bridge swung back.

"No," I lied a little.

"Most of 'em ah," he said. I imagined that he was disappointed that
he hadn't scared another invading camera-toting tourist.

Just past the bridge, I noticed the South Bristol Historical Society
on the left, a small white building set back from the road. *On the agenda
for tomorrow morning,* I thought. *There must be something I can learn there
about* Ellen Marie.

The hills challenged only a little in comparison to my expectations,
and sweet stillness once again cradled the rhythmic sound of my steps.

Chapter 8
South Bristol—Day 2

The weatherman reported a 70 percent chance of showers, but I didn't care. Wrapped in a tan slicker with blue cuffs, I traversed the steep driveway. Halfway down, I heard a deep, rasping birdcall that I didn't recognize. Looking up, I saw a magnificent, graceful heron and said, "So that's what you sound like!"

Cheryl from the B&B had suggested walking along the waterfront and Middle Road that connected with Route 129 by the church, so I turned right at the bottom of the driveway. Christmas Cove was so still that reflections of the skiffs, lobster boats, and sailboats were almost mirror-like in their perfection. Masts betrayed only the slightest rippling. Except in the shade of the trees, the cove looked white because of the overcast sky, but one strip of blue colored the distant waters. The road turned 90 degrees. On the other side of the restaurant, morning mist hung low. One lonesome hemlock on a tiny island close to shore pointed to blue sail covers that matched the strip of blue sky.

When the road turned inland, it split left and right. I chose to go left, not knowing which direction led to the church. I stopped to sit on a rock for a while at the edge of a tranquil fresh-water pond. Pink pond lilies emitted a delicate, sweet fragrance.

I knew I had taken the wrong road when, instead of the inland church, I viewed the harbor and the opposite shore. The distance across was so much greater than the expanse of the harbor near town that I feared I had made a grave mistake. I walked on. When I came upon Island Grocery, the sign for which I'd seen the day before, I was relieved. I knew its location was easy walking distance to and from the bridge. Past the store, I turned onto the familiar state road toward the historical society. When I arrived, the door was locked, and a sign indicated open hours from two to four in the afternoon.

I decided to return to Gamage's in hopes of finding Larry. Country music blared from a radio inside a modern blue shed to the left of the big gray building. The bay door was half open, so I passed between a sailboat and a large sloop to the rear of the shop. No one was there. When I walked around the other side of the sloop, I saw three men moving a boat in a mechanical sling on the other side of the yard. I didn't want to distract them from work that appeared to need concentration, so I walked to the building with the red roof at the end of the pier. No one was there. As I was about to leave, one of the men who had been moving the boat approached, so I told him that I was looking for Larry to see if he could tell me something about Harvey Gamage building *Ellen Marie,* the vessel I hoped to find.

"I haven't seen him today," the man, who was wearing a plaid shirt, told me, "but if you go out Shipyard Road there's a store to the left. Larry lives across from the store." I asked Larry's last name. It was Kelsey. I wasn't sure that dropping in unexpectedly was the right thing to do, but the man assured me that Larry would be delighted to talk about boatbuilding history anytime.

When I reached Larry's house, rather than approach the formal front door, I followed a flagstone path to a patio where, through screen and glass, I could see a trim woman dressed in jeans sitting on the couch. "Hello," I said, hoping not to startle her. Mrs. Kelsey took her sewing basket off her lap, set it on the couch, and approached the door to listen to my intrusion explanation. "Larry's upstairs on the computer," she said, holding the screen door ajar. "I'll tell him you're here."

I waited at a picnic table and stood when he arrived.

I was surprised by Larry's red hair and beard—he was too young to be familiar with boatbuilding in the early sixties, I thought. He remained standing as I clarified my *Ellen Marie*–related purpose. Although he was polite and informative, he didn't seem as anxious to talk about boats at this time as the man in the building with the red roof had led me to believe.

"I managed the Gamage Shipyard from 1971 to 1981," he said.

Larry told me that Mr. Gamage had had a basic plan for his fishing boats that could be lengthened or shortened according to what the buyer wanted to have built. By adding or deleting frames, the same basic plan could be built seventy feet long or a hundred feet long.

"When I was manager," he said," most of the boats built at the Gamage Yard were steel, but we built a few forty-foot wood boats. There were two bays in the big shed. Steel boats were built on one side and wood boats on the other. During my time, we built the *Appledore*, the *Bill of Rights*, and the *Harvey Gamage*. They were schooners."

Larry told me that I should talk with Dave Andrews, the town historian, about *Ellen Marie*. But he was away.

We remained standing during our entire conversation. It seemed that he'd rather be working at his computer, so I thanked him for his time and walked down the hill to Osier's.

"Mind if I sit a spell?" I asked the girl behind the counter.

"No. Help yourself," she replied.

I grabbed a soda from the cooler in the grocery section and took it to one of the heavily varnished tables across from the counter. A Bangor newspaper had been left on the other chair. I spread it out and scanned it.

Two fishermen, one a redhead and the other dressed in yellow oilers, were conversing near the counter. Apparently, the redhead had been observing the lobster boat piloted by the man in the oilers when a mate unwisely ventured onto the bow.

"Almost killed Jody on the bow," the redhead said matter-of-factly.

The fisherman in the oilers who had controlled the throttle said just as matter-of-factly in his slow Maine accent, "I was thinkin', *What do you s'pose he'd do if I cut bahk.*"

It took a while for my grin to subside.

The weather had cleared and turned warm. I bought some crabmeat and potato salad along with my soda, slung my slicker over my shoulder, and walked back to the B&B. When I got to Middle Road, I wondered how I had gone wrong before, so I turned right at the church. It made my trek twice as long as it had to be, but I was glad to become familiar with the route. When I got back, Sassy, the proprietors' golden retriever, kept me company while I ate my lunch on the deck.

Four ladies were researching genealogy around a table in the back of the small historical society room when I arrived at 2:30 p.m. "Is one of you Mrs. Wells?" I asked. An attractive woman with silver hair stood up. "Yes," she said. "I am." She felt sure that the historical society had nothing to contribute to my research about *Ellen Marie*. *There must be something*, I thought, looking around anyway. She said that I should speak with Nat Hammond for information about Gamage boats and Dave Andrews for information about boats in general.

"They should have lists of the boats built at the Gamage Yard," she said.

While Mrs. Wells looked for Nat Hammond's phone number, I looked at a photo of Harvey Gamage and read a 1966 Citation letter to him from Governor Curtis:

> The ancient craft of building wooden vessels lies at the very heart of our Maine heritage. Nowhere else in the world has this art been so fully and richly developed. The Homeric age of wooden ships belongs to our past. Yet here in Maine there remains one man to carry on with adze and calking iron this tradition. He has been building wooden ships since 1910. Through 1955 his yard in South Bristol built 75% of the New Bedford dragger fleet and a good share of the fishing vessels sailing out of Boston. In 1968, he launched the Antarctic research vessel, Hero, whose wood keel was the greatest timber laid down in our time. Then there was the schooner MARY DAY, and the magnificent topsail schooner, SHENADOAH, the last of the great wind ships. And only this past spring, CLEARWATER, a replica of last century Hudson River sloop, wet her bow in Maine waters.

This special Maine man is here today. For his contribution to our heritage and for his long history of excellence in the pursuit of his craft, it gives me great pleasure to present to Harvey Gamage, of South Bristol, Maine, a Maine State Award.

>   Cordially,
>   Kenneth M. Curtis
>   Governor

That certainly related to my research, I thought, impressed by the idea that the Gamage Yard had built 75 percent of the New Bedford dragger fleet.

With the phone to her ear, Mrs. Wells reported Nat Hammond's comments. "He says that he doesn't think he has anything you'd be interested in … He says that it's not likely that boats like *Ellen Marie* are still sailing." Mrs. Wells gave me Dave Andrews' e-mail address before I left.

Nat Hammond's disappointing comment slipped into a mental file labeled "Denial."

It was time to reflect. I'd been having a great time. I'd learned a lot but didn't want to know about boats in general. I wanted to find *Ellen Marie*, to know about *her*. I hoped to find her and stand on her deck. What did I need to do? *If I'm trying to find* Ellen Marie, I thought, *then I need to talk to a boat owner, maybe at Osier's, about boat registration.* That was my goal for tomorrow.

My legs were finally feeling the effects of hours of walking, and since it was my last night at the bed and breakfast, I took advantage of the Jacuzzi.

Chapter 9
South Bristol—Day 3

"Good luck finding *Ellen Marie*," Richard said as he and Cheryl, the B&B proprietors, waved good-bye. Intent on finding a fisherman to talk to, I drove toward Osier's, crossed the swing bridge, and slowed in front of the store, but there wasn't a place to park. I had wondered why a boat called *Charlotte C* had been left at risk inside the big dilapidated shed, so I continued to the shipyard to ask if there was an interesting story behind her presence. When I walked into the building with the red roof, five men were gathered together chatting. Steve, the man I had met there first, was not among them.

"I was wondering," I said. "Is there a story behind the *Charlotte C* being in the shed?"

"There isn't one," a man leaning against a shelf answered. The rest just stared at me.

I told them what I had heard about a Boothbay shipbuilder having bought the Yard.

"Naw. It's up for sale," the same man said.

"I heard a rumor that it was a done deal," I pressed. The answer was limited to one word: "Naw."

I was ill at ease. They might have been too. Who wouldn't have been suspicious of me? I carried a notebook and pen that probably inspired thoughts like *Danger: untrustworthy reporter.* They didn't know my motives, and I didn't offer them. I simply left and returned to Osier's.

The pretty girl with hazel eyes who had sold me the crabmeat the day before was crouching behind the varnished tables alternately spraying and wiping the paneling with a white cloth. I greeted her and asked who owned the draggers.

"David Osier," she said, standing to face me. "He owns all of this." Her arm swept a horizontal arc through the air, indicating that David owned the store as well as the boats.

"I'd like to talk with him," I told her. She turned without another word and walked to the back of the store and out the door to the deck. A few minutes later, she reported that David would be in shortly. She said her name was Stormy, and we chatted while she continued to polish the paneling.

David and I sat at one of the varnished tables and relaxed into easy conversation. I told him about *The Pilot House* and about my desire to see what South Bristol looked like and to learn what I could about *Ellen Marie*.

"How can I find her?" I asked. "Isn't there an agency that registers the fishing vessels?"

"National Marine Fisheries," he said, adding that if she had been sold, her name might have been changed. In that case, the permit, if it had been a federal scallop or fish permit, would have been redone.

I assured him that *Ellen Marie* was a groundfish dragger, not a scalloper. David reached into his pocket, put his wallet on the table, and pulled out his Northeast multispecies permit. He read a phone number from it that I wrote in my little blue notebook.

Our conversation expanded to the fishing industry—what I had heard about the limited fishing days and how difficult it was for a fishing-boat owner to make a go of it without multiple boats.

"I have five with a permit for forty-eight days," David said, "and two for fifty-nine days, and I'm not making it." He said that the crews did all right because they jumped from boat to boat. "It's expensive. Every four years an engine has to be rebuilt, and that costs twenty-five thousand dollars." The regulations, he explained, came from National Marine Fisheries Service (NMFS); he complimented the agency for doing a good job.

"Do the fishermen have a lobby?" I asked.

"The fishermen say one thing," he said. "The conservation groups sue; the judge looks at both sides and then decides." He told of an emergency calculation that was affecting him that didn't have to do with Maine fishermen but rather New Bedford and Gloucester fishermen who had caught too many cod. "The fish need to come back on paper and computer screens," he said.

David was so easy to talk with that I would have enjoyed a longer conversation, but I was sensitive to the value of his time, and besides, I had to get to Northport before lunch.

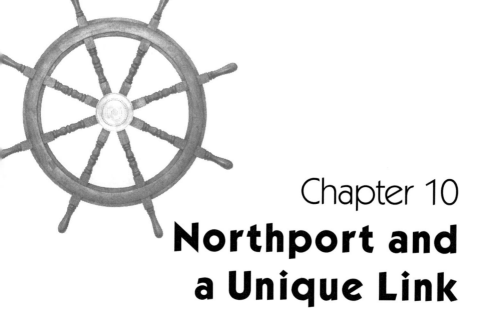

Chapter 10
Northport and a Unique Link

Mine was the only car on Bayside Road in Northport, so I slowed to a snail's pace to read printed MapQuest directions and look for street signs. As I approached a dirt road that angled away from the street at about one o'clock to my right, a brown-leashed vizsla with his nose to the ground trotted out of the side street. At the other end of the leash appeared Charlie Coupe, my former business associate and friend whom I'd planned to visit. His Bermuda shorts and floppy brimmed cap contrasted with the suit, shirt, and tie he always wore at the bank before he retired.

"Just keep going," Charlie said. "You'll find it. I'll meet you down there."

I grinned as I pulled in front of the blue and gray dome tent at the edge of the gravel parking area. The Coupes were in the process of building a house, and Charlie had teased that because the house was under construction, a tent would be my guest quarters. For a moment, I wondered if he had been serious, but the first-floor apartment they supplied was fabulous.

Charlie's wife, Elaine, insisted that I take the front seat in the pickup truck on our way to Belfast. "We're going to Young's," she said. "It's a great place for lobster." The place was a warehouse-like building, almost empty except for huge, waist-high lobster tanks that ran the length of the building on both sides of a center aisle. At the counter, I ordered boiled lobster, coleslaw, potato salad, and a cold drink. A heavyset young man in a white bib apron put a paper cup of melted butter on my tray, my lobster meat cradled in a paper dish, and plastic cutlery. Charlie and Elaine, carrying their own brown trays, led the parade down the aisle, through plastic strips at the wide doorway, and onto a deck where we ate in the sun overlooking Belfast harbor.

After lunch, we located Alden at Harbor Hill, the assisted-living facility where he lived. He was easy to identify from the description he had given me—the only one wearing a painter's hat in a power wheelchair. He balanced on his lap a large brown envelope that contained my copy of *The Dragger*, which he gave me in exchange for my twenty-dollar bill. Alden escorted us along paved walkways to a sunny garden area behind the building where we could sit, chat, and enjoy the view of the harbor. Charlie, Elaine, and Alden, who had designed electrical systems for yachts, conversed easily about the area and their experience with wooden boats. I clung to my package and listened until I was surprised by another coincidence. Alden's roots were in Fairhaven, Massachusetts.

That night, Charlie told me, as if it was a common occurrence, that his mother had been at the Gamage Yard in South Bristol for the launching of the schooner *Bill of Rights* and that he and Elaine had had their wedding reception aboard the schooner when it was moored in Newport, Rhode Island. Except for my purchase of *The Dragger*, I had expected my Northport visit to take me completely away from my *Ellen Marie* research. Now I was recognizing a link between it all. I began to wonder if the Gamage Yard was common knowledge to everyone but me—to everyone who knew anything about wooden boats, perhaps.

The next day Charlie and Elaine agreed to return to Young's before I left for Massachusetts. The plan was for me to follow them there in my car. But when I turned the key in the ignition, nothing happened. Not even a click.

"I've got a problem," I hollered up to Charlie, who was sitting in the driver's seat of his running truck.

Fixing my car had to become the priority, because as Charlie pointed out, it was Friday, and nobody in Maine worked on weekends. That evening, Gus, the local mechanic, explained his unsuccessful troubleshooting efforts and promised to get to work on it first thing Monday.

Elaine took me to Camden on Saturday while Charlie worked on the house. We wandered along the piers crowded with people and moored vessels. *Appledore II*, the schooner whose website I had visited when I searched for "Harvey Gamage Shipyard" in July, was next to the main quay. Near the ship, under a canopy, pamphlets and a photograph album enticed passersby to take a windjammer cruise. I flipped through the album's acetate pages, stopping at a photo depicting activity I wished I could have seen. The South Bristol historian had warned that it had not been the norm to photograph boats under construction, but before me, captured on film, were Harvey Gamage's carpenters building the *Appledore II* in the shed where *Ellen Marie* had been born.

The *Appledore* crew member who manned the table overheard me explain the photograph to Elaine. "You're familiar with the Harvey Gamage Yard?" he asked.

"Yes," I answered. "I'm researching a fishing vessel that was built there. I just spent a couple days in South Bristol. Have you been there?"

He said he hadn't but wished he had.

We took *Appledore* brochures and leisurely strolled under the clear blue sky to another pier where the Harvey Gamage schooner *Mary Day* was docked.

On Monday, Gus, the local mechanic, told us what he believed was wrong with my car but that it would have to go to the Toyota dealership in Rockland. The bundle of wires that caused the problem was finally replaced on Tuesday.

Before we left Northport to reclaim my car, I asked Charlie to tell me again how his mother happened to be at a Gamage Yard ship launching. To me, it was an amazing coincidence that both he and I had a connection to the Harvey Gamage Yard.

He explained that the son of one of his mother's childhood friends,

Joe Davis Junior, had commissioned the building of *Bill of Rights* and invited her to the launching.

"Why didn't you go?" I asked.

"I would have, but I was still away in the service."

I emailed Alden when I got home to say what a pleasure it had been to meet him and to tell him about the unintentional extension of my trip. "By the way," I added, "do you happen to know the fate of the *Ellen Marie* or know someone else, in Fairhaven, perhaps, who might have a clue to her whereabouts?"

Chapter 11
Calls to National Marine Fisheries and Massachusetts Division of Marine Fisheries

Back in Massachusetts, as soon as I thought offices would open, at nine o'clock, I dialed the National Marine Fisheries (NMF) phone number that David Osier had given me in hopes that someone could help me locate *Ellen Marie*. I was prepared, thanks to *The Dragger*, to report not only that she was a groundfish dragger built in South Bristol at the Harvey Gamage Yard in 1962 but also that her owner was Rudolph Matland and her captain was Woodie Bowers.

The woman who answered the call at NMF said that I needed to speak to Gerry Gaipo and transferred me to her answering machine. I left a message including the reason for my call and my home and office telephone numbers.

I tried my luck at a state office—the Massachusetts Division of Marine Fisheries. The state employee asked me if I knew the boatyard.

"No. That's why I'm calling," I answered. "I don't know where she is. I'm trying to find out what happened to her."

"Do you have a permit and registration number?"

"No. All I know is …" and I repeated the litany of *Ellen Marie* facts as I knew them.

"I wouldn't be able to access anything that old," the state worker said. "Those records are all packed away in the Brighton storage facility." She discouraged my inquiry into the records, saying that I would need the documentation number from the Coast Guard. Anyway, she thought that all they might have was a landing permit. She felt sure that *Ellen Marie* would have required a federal fishing permit because of the vessel's eighty-foot length. She said, "There's a seventy-two-foot cap to allow dragging in state waters."

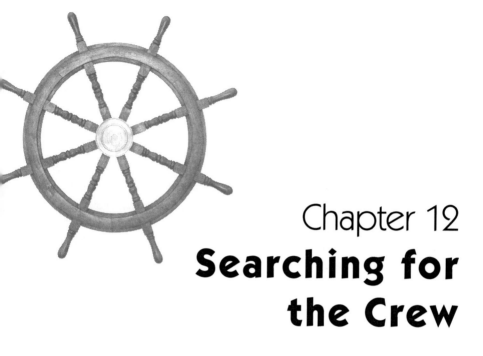

Chapter 12
Searching for the Crew

The Dragger listed the names of *Ellen Marie*'s crew when author William Finn had been a passenger in August of 1968. I wrote the names on a paper, intending to write phone numbers next to them if I found possible matches in the New Bedford phone book.

Captain Woodie Bowers
Tommy Barnes
Eddie Murphy
Eddie Ames
Paul Russo
Eddie Patenaude
Randy Conrad
George Hawley

The only potential match was a number for an Edward Patenaude in Fairhaven. I introduced myself to the woman who answered my call. "Is it possible," I asked, "that Mr. Patenaude is the Edward Patenaude who was on the dragger *Ellen Marie*?"

Her reply was slow and cautious. "Could be ..."

I was thrilled. A moment later, eighty-six-year-old Mr. Patenaude confirmed that he'd been *Ellen Marie*'s cook and explained how he'd become a fisherman.

"Being a western Massachusetts man, I had never seen the ocean until I joined the National Guard and was stationed at Camp Edwards. I met a girl at a USO dance and married her. She was a Norwegian girl from Fairhaven. Her father owned two fishing vessels. He introduced me to scalloping, and that was the beginning of a forty-two-year fishing career."

He didn't know what had happened to *Ellen Marie*.

I asked if Mr. Patenaude might enjoy perusing *The Dragger*. He liked the idea but said his wife was sick and we'd have to wait until she was feeling better.

Alden Trull had asked me to keep him informed if I learned anything interesting, so in an e-mail to him I shared my excitement about locating and talking with *Ellen Marie*'s cook. When I got his reply, I wasn't sure whose surprise was greater—his or mine. He said he was amazed that when reviewing *The Dragger*, his connection to Eddie Patenaude hadn't occurred to him. It turned out that one of Alden's high-school friends was Eddie Patenaude's son, Alan. They had shared a paper route and often had played basketball in Patenaude's driveway.

There seemed to be an unusual number of coincidences. I told Alden about a sign I had seen many years prior: "Coincidence is God's way of remaining anonymous."

Chapter 13
When Was that Federal Buyback?

If the *Angela W*, a sister ship to *Ellen Marie*, had been still afloat at the time of the federal buyback, then there was a chance that *Ellen Marie* had been afloat then too. All I needed to do was go back to the article in which I had first read about *Angela W*. The date should be there. An Internet search revealed two links. The first, the article I was looking for, was dated January 21, 1998. Since that was within ten years of my search, I concluded that there was a good chance that *Ellen Marie* was still around.

Out of curiosity, I clicked on the other link. It was an earlier 1966 *Standard Times* article about the buyout[8]—a great article for my purposes because it gave me names of several boat owners and other businessmen around New Bedford who might know what had happened to *Ellen Marie*. I remembered the hunch I had before going to South Bristol that studying the buyout would help me find her.

My first call was to Herbert Smith, who owned the *Curlew II* and

---

8   Jack Stewardson, "32 boats get buyout offers," *Standard-Times, South Coast Today*, http://www.southcoasttoday.com/daily/12-96/12-12-96/a011o004.htm

the *Mischief.* He didn't know what had happened to *Ellen Marie*, but he told me who he thought might know. "Lars Sovik is the one you should talk to," he said. I recognized the name, because it appeared just below Mr. Smith's in the buyback article.

Looking more closely at the article after I phoned Mr. Smith, I noticed a photo credit: "*Staff photo by Hank Seaman:* Herbert Smith … working in the hold of his Curlew II." Until then I had paid no attention to the photo, but after the call, I reflected on the fact that I knew what the man sounded like and had experienced his kindness. I had spoken with the man who until moments prior had been a stranger in a still photo. The connection felt mystical.

Another potential source of information from the buyout article was Kevin Ferreira, president of the Whaling City Seafood Display Auction. He also didn't know what had happened to *Ellen Marie*, but he tried to help. "Have you called the Whaling Museum?" He asked. "If she had sunk, they'd have a record." He also suggested calling Seaman's Bethel, which I did. The gentleman who answered suggested that I talk with Arthur Motta at the tourist office.

When I reached Lars Sovik and asked him about *Ellen Marie*, I received a fragment of encouraging information. "The last I knew she was sold and ended up on the Cape," he said. He mentioned a photographer of old boats who frequented the Ship Store where his wife, Sonja Sovik, worked. He passed the phone to Sonja, who told me that she had known *Ellen Marie*'s owner, Rudolph Matland. That revelation and the fact that she might have a photograph of *Ellen Marie* at the Ship Store fanned the flames of my passion.

"I'm there on Mondays and Saturdays," she said.

I wrote the store's address in my blue research notebook, Two Ferry Street in Fairhaven, intending to be there at the first opportunity.

I e-mailed Alden immediately and told him that I had spoken with Lars Sovik, owner of the *Valkyrie*, who thought that *Ellen Marie* had been sold to somebody on Cape Cod.

"Are you ready for another coincidence?" Alden replied. "Lars and his wife Sonja have lived in the same neighborhood where I grew up for the past thirty years or more, a stone's toss from my old house. Where next will your quest lead?"

Chapter 14
National Marine Fisheries—A Returned Call

It was Friday, September 22, when I received a call from Ted Hawes, a National Marine Fisheries employee in Gloucester. He'd heard from Gerry Gaipo, he said, after I left a message on her answering service.

"I can try to help," Ted said. "When was she built?"

I gave him the year, 1962, and *Ellen Marie*'s name when he asked.

"I'm doing a partial search," he said, followed by a few moments of dead air. "I have one built in 1961, seventy-five feet long."

When I commented on the difference in date, he said that it wasn't unusual to get discrepancies since the data came from the fishermen. "She was in Harwich and then in New Bedford. The hull number is 284313."

I asked for an owner's name, and Ted told me that Cape Oceanic Corporation was the entity that had owned the vessel in the mid-1980s. He suggested that I contact the Coast Guard for owner information and possibly obtain a title.

This glimmer of progress excited me. I was thankful for my recent visit with David Osier at the varnished table in South Bristol, Maine, where he had given me the phone number for National Marine Fisheries.

I hoped that the NMF data belonged to my *Ellen Marie*, but because of the difference in the year the boat was built and the length, which I thought should have been eighty feet, I wasn't completely convinced. I had to be sure.

Chapter 15
The Working Waterfront Festival

A familiar voice hollered my name. I turned and smiled as Jen Shepley walked toward me. I wondered how she had found me near the fishing boats at Steamship Pier when our rendezvous had been planned for a lecture tent near the visitors center two piers away.

We strolled up and down the pier where signs identified certain boats: Scalloper, Trawler. People boarded boats to tour them. I naïvely looked for a Dragger sign, because I wanted to step on the deck of a boat like *Ellen Marie*, but there was no Dragger sign and no look-alike vessel available to tour. I forgot my disappointment as Jen shared about having researched the fishing industry for an assignment when she was a high-school student in Mattapoisett, a waterfront town east of Fairhaven. I wished I had learned about the industry when I went to school in Wareham, another coastal town within a half-hour drive of New Bedford.

When we'd made our plans, I'd told Jen that I'd like to look for photos of *Ellen Marie* at the Ship Store in Fairhaven and visit the New Bedford Working Waterfront Festival. With lectures, films, food, music, and equipment demonstrations, there was plenty to do at the festival, but the Ship Store would close in an hour, so Jen and I decided to go there.

I introduced myself to the woman in a black, short-sleeve t-shirt behind the counter—Sonja Sovik, whom I'd spoken with by phone the week before. She pointed out the tall metal racks where photographs of *Ellen Marie* might be. Sonja, it seemed, could handle the cash register, help customers find the goods they sought, make a phone call, and have a conversation all at the same time. I was impressed by her energy and encouraged by her eagerness to help me. Jen and I looked through the racks of boat photographs while Sonja worked.

When Sonja's sister, Gail, the store owner, arrived, they chatted about relatives who might know about *Ellen Marie* and how to reach them. "Our mother's cousin married Mr. Matland," Sonja said, turning to me after she dialed the phone.

I remembered that Rudolph Matland had owned *Ellen Marie*. Their marriage connection excited my hope of gleaning information about my boat. Her attention returned to the phone quickly.

"Serena, what happened to Mr. Matland's boat, the *Ellen Marie*?"

Sonja put the receiver down and turned to report that *Ellen Marie* had been sold to a man in Hyannis. She didn't know any more. In between tasks, Sonja dialed the phone again to try to reach the photographer Steve Kennedy, who might have photographed *Ellen Marie*. He didn't answer, but she vowed to try again.

After thumbing through the photographs without finding any of *Ellen Marie*, Jen and I perused the store's wares—imported Norwegian food, sweatshirts, knickknacks, fishermen's gear, Norwegian sweaters, boots, and bumper stickers. When we returned to the counter, Sonja suggested that I talk with Woodie Bowers.

"He's still around?" I asked, surprised because of my limited success at locating crew members.

"Oh yes. I'll give you his number." She plopped the New Bedford phone directory onto the counter and began flipping pages. I could have told her that his number wasn't there. She promised to get it to me.

I drove Jen back to her car in New Bedford but was not ready to abandon my efforts for the day. The quiet walk to the Whaling Museum seemed lonely in the late afternoon compared to the lively waterfront, but the museum was active. A knowledgeable employee gave me the business card of the assistant librarian at the research library. My passion drove me further to the public library, where I scanned the computerized catalog until I surrendered to the waning of time.

The following day, Sunday, although I wanted to be in New Bedford, I followed through with plans I'd made to rendezvous with a friend at a blues festival in Middleboro. Another friend, Jane Marsh, who happened to be at the same event, shared her program, in which I read the lyrics of tunes that the next band would sing. They were dark lyrics—a style that intensified my I-don't-want-to-be-here feeling. I felt as agitated as a corralled wild horse. I apologized for not staying long and left for the Working Waterfront Festival.

I wanted to hear Richard Adams Carey talk about his book *Against the Tide: The Fate of the New England Fisherman.* I had been compassionately interested in the topic ever since I first heard about the forty-eight-day limit and the near demise of the fishing industry in South Bristol, Maine. Mr. Carey was scheduled to speak at the narrative stage on Fisherman's Wharf from 2:00 to 2:45 p.m. I was late. He was answering a question about caviar when I arrived. The audience apparently was interested in Mr. Carey's other book, *The Philosopher Fish: Sturgeon, Caviar, and the Geography of Desire.* A schedule keeper with a clipboard approached the platform to encourage the participants to bring the conversation to an end. I wandered into the adjacent bookstore, where I purchased a hardcover copy of *Against the Tide* and another book, *Vanishing Species: Saving the Fish, Sacrificing the Fisherman,* by Susan R. Playfair. Above his name, Mr. Carey inscribed my copy of *Against the Tide:* "For Rachel, in hopes of good fortune in her quest for the *Ellen Marie.*"

It was getting late. The opportunity to experience the diversity of the festival was slipping away. I sat in the audience while New Bedford Harbor Commissioner Rodney Avila delivered questions from fishermen to representatives of government regulatory agencies. From what I gleaned, it seemed to me that there needed to be more communication between the government and the fishermen. The festival's final half hour slipped by as I listened to the New Bedford Sea Chantey Chorus and took a quick tour of an orange steel scalloper, the interior of which looked and felt as comfortable as an apartment.

Chapter 16
A Special Day

In the few minutes I had before needing to leave for work, I dialed 411 for a number for Cape Oceanic Corporation. That was the *Ellen Marie* owner that National Marine Fisheries employee Ted Hawes had told me about. It was worth a try even though the year built and the vessel length of the *Ellen Marie* in the NMF files were slightly different from those I thought were my *Ellen Marie*'s. Directory assistance gave me a number.

The recorded message on the answering machine identified Cape Coastal Builders. I assumed that directory assistance had made a mistake. Annoyed, I redialed 411, enunciated Cape Oceanic Corporation as clearly as I could, and even spelled *c-a-p-e*, which of course confused the computer and switched me to an actual operator. Again I requested the telephone number for Cape Oceanic Corporation. I was given the same number. This time, when the Cape Coastal Builders answering machine connected, I explained how I got the number and said, "I'm calling because I bought a painting of a fishing dragger named *Ellen Marie*, and I have this overwhelming desire to learn what happened to her. If someone there can help me, I'd appreciate a call." I left my phone number.

My negative thinking kicked in. What was the likelihood that somebody at a construction office would have information about *Ellen Marie*? If someone there knew about *Ellen Marie*, why would that person spend his or her time on something that was important to *me?* I left the results to a higher power and headed to work. Around midday, I answered the phone, never thinking that the call might be about *Ellen Marie*, but the caller referenced the message I had left that morning. The first thing I wanted to do was make sure we were talking about the same *Ellen Marie*. "Was she owned by Rudolph Matland?" I asked. She was. "And your name again is what?"

"Jim Spalt."

Mr. Spalt had purchased *Ellen Marie* in 1980. "She was nice," he said, "but she didn't have enough power to compete." He explained that he had replaced her original 365-horsepower engine with a 510-horse-power engine from another Gamage boat, the *Explorer*. Mr. Spalt said that the previous owner had converted her to scalloping. When he said something about adding a boom to her, I cringed, because it reminded me of the *Candy B II's* top-heavy condition after a boom was added—the possible cause of her loss. I hoped *Ellen Marie* hadn't suffered a similar fate.

"She was upgraded but very sound," he continued. "I made a lot of money with her, so I was able to buy larger steel boats."

"What did you do with her?" I asked.

"That's a long story," he said with a sigh. But he didn't stop there. He educated me about rules and regulations, a scallop-size law, regula-tions about how much shellfish you can take, violation notices, records inspections, litigation, and his experience with all of it that led to a forced choice of either liquidation or seizure. His had been the first violation notice that the government issued in its efforts to enforce the new regu-lations. He had been wiped out, so *Ellen Marie* had to be sold.

I told Mr. Spalt about my first exposure to the regulations when I was in South Bristol, and I told him about my being drawn to the orange mast and the orange lifeboat in *The Pilot House*.

"It was definitely orange," he affirmed. "I took it off her before I sold her. I sold her to a man named Bronko in Rhode Island."

"Bronko?"

"That's what they called him. I don't remember his last name. He fished out of New Bedford and then Newport, or maybe New Jersey. I think she eventually sank around 1989 or 1990."

I wanted to ignore those last disheartening words, but I thought again about the added boom and wondered if she had iced up and rolled like the *Candy B II*. Maybe nothing had happened to her at all. Maybe the idea that *Ellen Marie* had sunk was just a mistake. I hoped so.

Ellen Marie in Hyannis, photographed by Steve Kennedy

Chapter 17
The Connections

Sonja Sovik phoned the same day that Jim Spalt returned my call. She sounded excited to share Capt. Bowers' phone number and some information that someone had passed on to her. She had heard that *Ellen Marie*'s name had been changed to the *Three Vs* and that she might have sunk around 1985. I didn't have the heart to tell her that I had already heard about the possible sinking.

I sent a progress report to Alden to tell him about the calls from National Marine Fisheries, Jim Spalt, and Sonja. The phone number on David Osier's fishing permit, it turned out, had been a key to progress.

Alden expressed fascination with the stories and coincidences surrounding *The Pilot House*. He recognized that I could have purchased *The Dragger* from many online sites, but because I had chosen to buy it from him, he had been able to experience the intrigue. The morning I received his response, I too had been contemplating the coincidences and connections.

The phone rang. It was Jane, my friend who had been at the blues concert the second day of the Working Waterfront Festival. I explained that I had left the concert because I'd never been clearer about the value of time and that the Working Waterfront Festival was important to me. Passion for my quest for *Ellen Marie* bubbled over into our conversation. I said, "I'm telling you, Jane, this whole thing has just grabbed me. I've learned so much. I had no idea what was going on in the fishing industry. When I was in South Bristol, I learned that the government is limiting fishing days to forty-eight—forty-eight days out of three hundred sixty-five. How can the fishermen possibly survive? The government is trying to bring back the fish population. I can understand that, but the fishermen are victims ..."

"I know," Jane interjected. "The scientists want to get the fishermen involved."

I was stymied by her words. I hadn't expected her to understand. Then I remembered that Jane had been employed at the Woods Hole Oceanographic Institute.

After hanging up with Jane, I further contemplated the connections. Why had the color orange drawn me so strongly to a painting of a fishing vessel when, at the time I purchased it, I had no particular interest in commercial fishing or boats? Why had this passion to find *Ellen Marie* developed? Was it likely that friends I knew through banking, Charlie and Elaine, would be familiar with the Gamage Yard and one of Harvey Gamage's vessels? And what were the chances that I would find my coveted copy of *The Dragger* in Maine, close to Charlie and Elaine, sold by a Fairhaven, Massachusetts, native? And if Alden hadn't expressed interest in my search for *Ellen Marie*, we would never have enjoyed the coincidences related to the Soviks and the Patenaudes.

The coincidences reminded me of something special that I had heard and seen at Boston's Park Street Church in the 1970s. Corrie ten Boom, a Dutch Christian woman, had helped Jews escape from Hitler's hunters until she was caught and incarcerated in Ravensbrook concentration camp. Since her miraculous release from the camp, she had been speaking around the world about God's saving love. When she spoke in Boston, that elderly lady, soft-spoken with a gray pompadour and rimless glasses, held up the back side of a tapestry for the audience to see. Long pieces of thread—red, blue, yellow, black, brown, green, purple—hung in disarray. She explained that the pieces of thread were like life—some parts dark, some not so dark—that we didn't understand because we looked from the back side. As she spoke the word *but,* she turned the tapestry around to reveal a magnificent floral design. Oohs and ahs resonated from all over the audience. She continued to say that God sees the other side, where together the threads make a beautiful pattern.

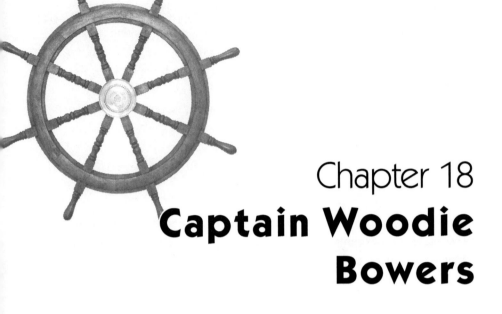

Chapter 18
Captain Woodie Bowers

When I contemplated calling Captain Woodie Bowers, I suddenly questioned my mission. *What am I doing?* I thought. *I'm about to call the Captain of the Ellen Marie and ask him what?* I felt vulnerable, small, and insignificant, like a curious nobody daring to approach this iconic man who had courageously battled the seas and directed the crew on the *Ellen Marie*, a man I feared might dismiss my inquiry as easily as flicking a fly off a lapel.

My courage returned after I focused on my desire to learn the fate of *Ellen Marie*, so I made the call. Mrs. Bowers answered. When Sonja Sovik had given me the number, she had suggested that I explain to Mrs. Bowers the reason for my call and that the phone number had come from Sonja. So I did.

"You want to know about the *Ellen Marie?*" Mrs. Bowers double-checked.

"Yes," I said. "That's right."

"I better let you talk to him."

So I talked to the man I feared and had put on a pedestal, Captain Woodie Bowers. In a raspy voice, Captain Bowers said that he wasn't sure what had happened to *Ellen Marie*. He'd heard that she might have caught fire off Block Island and sunk. Our conversation could have been that brief, but much to my delight, the captain told a longer story.

"I was on the boat seventeen years," he said. "I brought her down from Maine when she was new."

I grabbed a pen and settled in with the phone to my ear to listen like a child at a storyteller's feet.

"The boat was built for Joseph Perry. He was a contractor. I asked him to get a boat for me." I noted Perry's name on the white lined pad on the desk. "Harvey Gamage had this boat already started. Perry bought the boat right then. He sent me up to South Bristol to see Mr. Gamage to tell him how I wanted the boat finished out. I took her out for a trial run and then brought her home."

The words played out like a movie in my mind, thanks to my recent experience in South Bristol.

"It was just a matter of months," he continued. "Mr. Perry went to Florida and died. That's when Rudolph Matland bought it. I was on her for seventeen years," he repeated. "Then I took a vacation. She was sold, but I don't know who she was sold to."

I told Captain Bowers about finding Cape Oceanic Corporation in Hyannis.

"I made a lot of improvements in the forecastle," he said, referring to the crew's quarters. "I put a refrigerator in place of the old icebox, and I put in hot and cold water for the cook."

I told him about boarding a scalloper, one of the big steel boats, during the Working Waterfront Festival and how surprised I had been that the forecastle was as nice as a modern apartment kitchen.

"Those old wood boats compared to boats of today," he said, "that's like going from a cave to a castle. The old piers, the old buildings where fish were unloaded—they're all gone. Things became so much different when they started building steel boats—the stern trawlers."

Captain Bowers patiently explained, "*Ellen Marie* was an either-side side trawler. The nets were taken up over the side."

I failed to grasp some of his explanation, because I was unfamiliar with terminology. I thought he said that quarter loops would take up the belly part of the net but the wings would stay out. I didn't ask for clarification.

"On the stern trawlers," he continued, "the whole net goes up on the spool. It's simple—easy."

I thanked Captain Bowers and left my phone number with the hope that he might locate and want to share some pictures of *Ellen Marie* from collections that he said had been passed on to his children.

Chapter 19
Arthur Motta

The following week, I took my camera to the New Bedford Visitors Center to photograph the fisherman's portrait and *Ellen Marie*'s column on the fish auction blackboard. I knew because of a similar identified picture in *The Dragger* that the silk-screen portrait was of Captain Bowers. I also planned to talk with the director of tourism, Arthur Motta, whom someone at Seamen's Bethel had suggested I contact.

Mr. Motta, relaxed in khakis and a crisp, short-sleeved shirt, did not know what had happened to *Ellen Marie*, but he tried to do everything he could, it seemed, to help me find out. He brought forth a list that we scanned together of boat losses in which there had been fatalities. *Ellen Marie* wasn't there.

"If you go over to the Harbor Development Commission, they might have some information," he suggested. I didn't tell him that I had already been there. Mr. Motta told of a photographer, John Ryan, who might have taken pictures of *Ellen Marie* as he photographed boats going through the hurricane barrier, and he recommended that I contact Fairhaven's harbormaster, who collected berthing fees.

"The Coast Guard has a database of all sinkings," he said. "You could contact them in Woods Hole. Tell them that you're doing historical research. And there are archival photos on the National Marine Fisheries website."

Having exhausted all of his other ideas, Mr. Motta offered to run the visitor center's fishing video, which included footage of some old boats. As he started the machine, he mentioned some of the fishermen in the film: "Jens Isaakson and John Isaakson ..."

I thought, *These must be names that anyone with even a shallow connection to New Bedford fishing would know.* I felt vulnerable being so ignorant.

In the black-and-white film, boats that looked like *Ellen Marie* plowed through moderate seas accompanied by high-pitched narration reminiscent of the sometimes-tremulous newsreels of the 1950s. Men in heavy plaid shirts, boots, and loose-fitting oilers lifted nets, operated winches, and packed fish on ice while the chronicler described the process that ended at the docks, where lumpers unloaded the catch.

At the conclusion of the film, I reconsidered Mr. Motta's suggestion that I try the Harbor Commission. Now that I knew *Ellen Marie*'s hull number, a revisit was a good idea.

Portrait of Captain Arnold "Woodie" Bowers and *Ellen Marie*'s column in the fish auction display in the New Bedford Visitors Center

Chapter 20
Shelly

When I returned to the New Bedford Harbor Commission, the same receptionist who had assisted me when I visited with Marie six weeks earlier greeted me. Her dark blond hair was pulled back except for deep, separated bangs that arched over her forehead. I began to describe our first visit.

"Oh yes," she said with a smile. "I remember you."

I told her that I now had the hull number for *Ellen Marie* and asked if it would be too much trouble to use it in another search. Shelly was happy to help. As she typed the number into the computer, she reiterated, "Documentation numbers always stay the same—with the boat. Here it is. It's coming up as the *Three Vs*, but it doesn't give any other information."

"That's the name I was told it was changed to," I said. "I've heard that it might have sunk in the mid-eighties. Does it give the owner?"

"Little Fishery Inc., but that's all." She handed me a printout and told me that I could find this information myself if I wanted to. She gave me the website and some phone numbers for the Coast Guard.

"I'm really curious about this now," Shelly said. "Any time I hear about a boat that sank, I want to know what happened."

"Do you come from a fishing family?" I asked.

"Yes, my dad was a fisherman, my husband is, and my son is. I lost my dad when his boat went down."

"What?" I was shocked.

Shelly explained. "He radioed that he was coming in, that he was running into a squall, but he was all right. My mother went to the pier to meet him, but he didn't come in. It was my daughter's birthday. The Coast Guard searched for a day, but they didn't find anything. My husband knew I couldn't live with not knowing. He was determined to find them."

The word *them* motivated me to ask if there had been a crew.

"My father and his partner," she answered. "My husband wouldn't give up. He kept looking and finally found them. Then the state police dive team took over and recovered the bodies."

"My God. I'm so sorry."

"That's why I'm interested when I hear that a vessel sank," Shelly continued. "I want to know what happened." She hesitated a moment. "You know the danger, but you think, *It will never happen to me.* He loved my kids. He used to want to take my son out with him, and I'd express my concern. He would say, 'I'd never let anything happen to him.' 'But nature …' I'd say. 'You can't control nature.'"

Shelly said that the tragedy had happened in 1994.

"What was the name of your father's boat?" I asked.

"The *Wanderer*," she said. Shelly had maintained eye contact and shared her experience somberly without other discernible emotion—the gift, perhaps, of twelve years having passed.

"This is our project now," I said. "I'll tell you whatever I learn." In my car outside the Harbor Commission office, I jotted a few notes about what Shelly had said. I shook my head, deeply moved by the experience, and prayed, "God, please surround that girl with love!"

Coincidentally, Shelly and I had met when we did because of an advertisement I'd seen for the harbor cruise in a publication called the *Wanderer.*

Chapter 21
The *Rianda*

Before I left the Harbor Commission office, one of its employees, Tommy Vital, entered the room. Shelly told him about my *Ellen Marie* research.

"There aren't many boats left like her," Tommy said. "One of them is *Rianda*. You should go over to see her. She's tied up next to McLean's in Fairhaven."

I wasn't sure whether to search for *Rianda* or go straight back to work. Curiosity won. I turned right off Route 6 onto Middle Road in Fairhaven. The stern-located wheelhouse of an eastern rig caught my attention. When I drove onto the pier, I could see her name, *Rianda*, painted red in a white stripe on her bow. Because it was low tide and most of her hull was hidden below the dock, I couldn't get a great look at her. The dock that would give me such a view was closed off by a heavy chain and a warning sign: Private Pier. I wanted to step over the chain, but a man standing on the pier was looking my way.

"Is this *your* pier?" I asked when he finished a cell-phone call. He said that it was.

"Is it all right if I walk on?"

He invited me to do so. I introduced myself and said, "I'm looking for a good vantage point to photograph the *Rianda*."

"Warren Alexander," he said as he extended his hand to shake mine.

"The best place to do that is up on the deck." He immediately led the way toward his *Ocean Princess* tied up at the end of the pier. "I have eighteen scallopers and four more coming up. They just launched another ship in Alabama. That's who I was talking to on the phone."

"Congratulations! Do you skipper one of the boats?"

"No. I'm too busy in administration," he said. "I miss the fishing."

Rianda's pilot house was broader than *Ellen Marie's* and elevated, and she looked longer than *Ellen Marie's* eighty feet. I pretended to be unaffected, photographing her nonchalantly, but inside I was thrilled to be on the deck of the *Ocean Princess* and grateful for the privilege.

"There aren't many boats left like her," Tommy
said. "One of them is *Rianda*."

Chapter 22
Photos

In a message on my answering machine, Shelly from the New Bedford Harbor Commission said that her step-dad, Rodney Avilla, had put photos of *Ellen Marie* on a disk for me. "They're black and white, most of 'em," she said. "Some are of men on the boat fishing. He has a book about the *Ellen Marie* too, but he couldn't find it. I have the disk here. You can pick it up the next time you're in the area."

She must have been referring to *The Dragger*. The photos in the book were black and white, so I thought perhaps someone had photographed the pages, but she said that some were in color. Not only was I curious to see what was on the disk, but I was amazed that Rodney would go to the trouble to provide it for me. He must have been motivated by Shelly's interest in my *Ellen Marie* research.

When I got home with the disk the next day, I went immediately to the computer. Two file names appeared in my Picture Project software: "Ellen Marie II" and "Ellen Marie Photos." The pictures in the first file I opened were not photos of book pages; the quality and composition of most were similar to the book photographs, but they were not duplicates. They appeared to be a collection that William Finn, the author of *The Dragger*, might have taken but not included in the book. Others appeared to be of *Ellen Marie* after she was converted to scalloping. Flabbergasted,

I scrolled through the second file. Not only were there twenty-five photographs that without much doubt had been taken by William Finn, but the set included the portrait of Captain Woodie Bowers that was featured in the New Bedford Visitors Center.

Why? I wondered. *Why have these treasures fallen into my possession? Why am I so privileged?*

Chapter 23
The Coast Guard

Late Wednesday afternoon, October 6, I received a phone call at work from someone who identified herself as Hollynn Kidwell of the Coast Guard's National Vessel Documentation Center. She wanted to verify my fax machine number, because her attempts to fax the abstract of title had been unsuccessful.

I told her that the number was correct. "I'm walking upstairs to the machine as we speak," I said. Officer Kidwell waited patiently as I randomly pushed fax-machine buttons.

"I suppose you're anxious to leave for the day," I said to Ms. Kidwell.

"I'm here until five thirty," she said. "I could try it again before I go home. If it doesn't go through, I'll try it again in the morning."

We hung up after I apologized for the inconvenience and thanked her for her patience. I almost groaned with frustration as I searched for the solution in the fax-machine manual and turned words into action that would correct the problem. I wanted that report! I didn't know what time it was, but it felt very close to five thirty.

The fax machine rang three times while I was troubleshooting. *Acceptance is the answer to all my problems today. Everything is the way it should be for the moment*, I repeated mentally—a valuable mantra I had learned from a special book. It helped to calm my nerves. Finally, the familiar word *sleep* appeared in the message window of the fax machine, meaning that it was functioning normally again.

Probably too late, I thought, *but at least it's fixed.*

At 5:16 p.m., the fax machine rang, followed by the familiar sound of the machine revving up to print. Seconds later, the upside-down page of whatever was being printed poked out of the delivery chute. I lifted it and read, "Department of Homeland Security US Coast Guard."

Yes! At last! I held in my hands an official document of my *Ellen Marie.* Under the bold heading "General Index or Abstract of Title," I read the information that had been entered on the fill-in-the blank lines: "This vessel was built at South Bristol, Maine in 1961 of wood by Harvey F. Gamage, builder for Boat Ellen Marie, Inc. as appears by Master Carpenter's Certificate of Harvey F. Gamage."

I remembered that the build date that Ted Hawes from National Marine Fisheries had had for *Ellen Marie* was 1961. The conflicting 1962 date that I'd given him had been wrong. A year difference in build date hadn't been surprising to Ted, because the information had been supplied by the fisherman. In this case, the fisherman, Woodie Bowers, had given the correct year to the NMF.

The *a* in the word *carpenter's* fell below the level of the other letters—evidence that it had been typed on a manual typewriter by an imperfect typist as most documents were in the 1960s.

There were four pages, nine columns, and twenty-six lines of information that weren't at first easily decipherable. I'd expected names of individuals and addresses that would make it easy to find *Ellen Marie.* The lack of this kind of information was disappointing. The document gave me the owners' names, but with one exception, they were all corporations. There were no corporate officers listed and no addresses. Regardless, I was determined to study the document and cull from it every usable bit of information. To begin, I had to refresh my memory of the words *grantor* and *grantee*—which one was buyer and which one was seller. The document contained mortgage information. In 1961, *Ellen Marie* had been purchased for $55,000. Cape Oceanic Corporation had purchased her in 1980 for $330,000. That was Jim Spalt, the owner who had suffered the consequences of regulations infractions. When he had liquidated in 1985, he apparently had sold her to "Bronko" for $165,000.

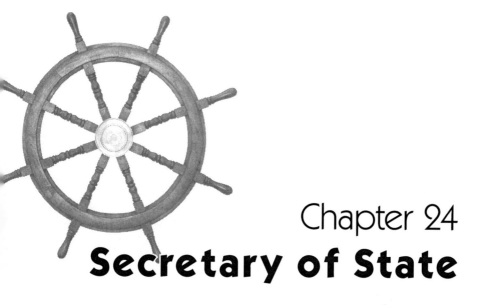

Chapter 24
Secretary of State

Researching *Ellen Marie*'s corporate owners on the Massachusetts Secretary of State's website was as gratifying as a generous paycheck after a hard week's work. On the computer screen, under the commonwealth's blue and yellow state seal, appeared the summary of the corporation Boat Ellen Marie Inc. Because it listed no corporate officers, I could only continue to assume that Joseph Perry, the contractor whom Captain Bowers had told me about, was at least one of the incorporators. The corporation, according to the summary, had been dissolved in 1963, two years after Perry bought her. The date of organization, July 7, 1978, didn't make sense. It must have been a data-entry error, I thought, until I realized, after further study of the title, that Boat Ellen Marie Inc. was not only *Ellen Marie*'s first owner but also her fourth. Perhaps 1978 was a reorganization date, but with Mr. Perry dead, who could have reorganized it? That was a mystery but not without a clue. The summary provided the location of the corporation's office: 2 Middle Street, Fairhaven. I found six businesses at that address in the Internet's white pages directory, none of which had a name remotely resembling Boat Ellen Marie Inc. That wasn't surprising considering that forty years had passed. I kept the mystery in the back of my mind; I had a hunch that Sonja Sovik could shed some light on it.

Success continued with the printing of the summary for Matland Fishing Corporation, *Ellen Marie*'s second owner. Matland owned her for fifteen years, from August of 1962 until July of 1977—the time during which Woodie Bowers made his and *Ellen Marie*'s reputation as a high-liner. This summary gave me names and addresses. It listed the president, Rudolph K. Matland; the treasurer, Rudolph B. Matland; and the secretary, Sharon J. Matland.

It was impossible to research *Ellen Marie*'s third owner in the corporate information because it was an individual, James S. Taylor, who bought her from Matland Fishing Corp. in July of 1977. He owned her only until the following July, when he sold her to the second Boat Ellen Marie Inc.

Owners five and six were Cape Oceanic Corp. and Ellen Marie Corp., both run by James Spalt, president, and Peter Spalt, treasurer. *Ellen Marie* was under the Spalts' Cape Oceanic Corp. ownership from March of 1980 and under the Spalts' Ellen Marie Corp. ownership from November of 1982 until they sold her, as Mr. Spalt put it, "to a man named Bronko," who must have been an officer in Little Fishery Inc., the corporation listed on the title.

A search of Rhode Island secretary of state records gave me a corporation ID number, 34922, for Little Fishery Inc. and a telephone number for the Rhode Island Corporations Division. I called.

"If I give you the corporate ID," I asked, "can you give me the principals involved?" I wanted Bronko's real name. "Unfortunately, no," said the clerk. "The computers are down." My plan to search for Bronko was thwarted, but she suggested that she might be able to help the following day.

I tried to track down James Taylor, *Ellen Marie*'s third owner—the one between Matland and Spalt. The title indicated that Plymouth had been her port under Taylor's ownership, so I contacted the Plymouth Harbormaster and the Plymouth Environmental Police. Neither entity was able to help.

Ellen Marie's owners:

1) Boat Ellen Marie Inc.   Joseph Perry

2) Matland Fishing Corporation   Rudolph Matland

3) James Taylor

4) Boat Ellen Marie Inc.   ?

5) Cape Oceanic Corp   James Spalt

6) Ellen Marie Corp.   James Spalt

7) Little Fishery Inc.   "Bronko"

Chapter 25
Another Conversation with Captain Woodie Bowers

It occurred to me that I didn't know how *Ellen Marie* got her name, so I called Captain Bowers again to ask him.

"Joseph Perry ..." Captain Bowers thought out loud. "I think Ellen Marie was his daughter's name."

He shifted into a more detailed *Ellen Marie* story. I grabbed paper and pen and practiced my shorthand. "When the boat was being built up in Maine," he said, "it was built on spec. I had asked him to get a boat for me. He called Gamage. Gamage had started with the planking. Mr. Perry sent me up with one of his drivers. He had three other boats scalloping. This was a dragger. When she was launched, we were sent up to bring the boat down. We took a trial run. Everything seemed okay. A Caterpillar man was sent with me to check the engine coming down. When she was ready, we came to New Bedford. All the buoys were gone in Buzzards Bay—the channel buoys. Ice took the buoys out. I went by landmarks."

I was awestruck by his sailing prowess. Yet there was not a hint of grandiosity in his telling of the facts. I told him that I had gotten a copy of *Ellen Marie's* title from the Coast Guard and that I had all the names of *Ellen Marie's* owners. "Do you know James Taylor?" I asked.

"James Taylor bought her after my seventeen years. He was from somewhere on Cape Cod. Had one small boat. I had gone away to China. I went to Hong Kong. I ran a few trips with Jimmy Taylor. She didn't have the power for scalloping."

I told him about Mr. Spalt putting another engine in her. "When you think of the *Ellen Marie*," I asked, "what's the first thing that comes to your mind? Were there particularly memorable experiences—storms maybe?"

"With the boat, everything went along." I knew he meant that *Ellen Marie* gave him no problems, but then he said, "I had a man that was killed on the winch, and another fell overboard."

I regretted that out of my naïveté I had asked an elderly gentleman to relive painful memories. It hadn't occurred to me that something this serious might have happened.

He continued, "He was told over and over, 'Don't handle the rope that way.' I had come forward to get a cup of coffee. I had to give the wheel to the mate. While I was pouring my coffee, I heard a thump. He got snarled up. His body was laying on the winch. His head was along-side—taken right off. There was nothing you could do or say. I got on the phone, let the boat stay still, and reported to the Coast Guard. They told me to proceed to Woods Hole. The owner met us there. The Coast Guard took all the stories. It wasn't the boat's fault. The other one … we was in a gale of wind. The engineer wanted to check if the bilge pump was working all right. He went overboard. One of the crew jumped in and got him, but he couldn't hold onto the guy."

"I hope I didn't upset you by bringing these things up," I said.

I felt comforted when he responded, "It was a long time ago."

"If you wanted the kids today to know something about fishing, what would it be?"

"When they came out with these stern trawlers, they were so much better—better conditions, less work for the crew, the way the nets come in."

I said, "You're quite a celebrity, you know. Why is that?"

"I guess because I'm one of the high-line captains."

"What does that mean?" I had been unsure of that term for a while and was glad to have it defined by Captain Bowers.

"That is the guy that lands the most fish and the crew that makes the most money." He hesitated a moment and changed the subject. "I found a few papers. I'll see what else I can find and get in touch. Call any time I can help."

Chapter 26
Dave Andrews

I don't know why I waited so long to contact Dave Andrews, the historian whose e-mail address Mrs. Wells had given me when I visited South Bristol. I sent him a message on the same day that I talked with Captain Bowers for the second time. I asked Mr. Andrews if he knew how I could find *Ellen Marie*–related Shipyard records—anything, but particularly photos of her being built or her launching photos.

When I read that he had attached a sea-trial photo to his response, I could have leapt out of my chair. He included his data sheet on *Ellen Marie* as well. Unfortunately, he didn't have launching photos; to his knowledge, photos of work in progress weren't often taken. He said that there were no surviving records from the Harvey Gamage Shipyard and called that a great pity. I agreed.

"Your boat," Dave wrote, "was one of many similar eastern-rig draggers built by Harvey Gamage from the late 1940s to the early 1970s. I would see what you could find out about her in New Bedford."

He had no way of knowing what the extent of my sleuthing had been. He suggested that I get a copy of *The Dragger* by William Finn and Peter Prybot's *White-Tipped Orange Masts: Gloucester's Fishing Draggers, 1970-1972 A Time of Change.* I didn't know about that one and appreciated the recommendation, because it would provide background on the draggers.

He offered assistance if I wanted to know more about the Gamage Yard and mentioned that the Whaling Museum in New Bedford had a model of the *Albatross,* a dragger similar to Ellen Marie and built by Gamage about the same time.

Because Dave was actively collecting data on vessels built in South Bristol, he welcomed a copy of any *Ellen Marie* information I might find. I was able to forward something that very day, because concurrently with receiving his e-mail, I received one from Laura Pereira, the assistant librarian at the New Bedford Whaling Museum Library. She had found three color images of *Ellen Marie* taken by Norman Fortier and a small collection of photos taken by William Finn, all of which could be found on the Whaling Museum's website. She wrote, "The Fortier images can be viewed through the museum's website, www.whalingmuseum. org. Select Collections Search and then Search Photo Archives." I used "Ellen Marie" as the keyword search term.

At a later time, I asked if Dave had noticed the differences between *Ellen Marie*'s sea-trial photo and the painting. I had previously sent him a picture of *The Pilot House.* To me, the most noticeable difference had been that there was only one lifeboat in the painting. There were two in the sea-trial photo—one on each side of the wheelhouse. I wondered why one boat would have been removed.

Dave said that almost all of the Gamage boats had two dories that had been built, like the fishing boats, in South Bristol. He speculated that Coast Guard rules might have changed to require more efficient release of the safety vessel, perhaps referring to what appeared to me to be an inflatable raft on *Ellen Marie*'s port side. He thought that the 1970s Gamage boats had a single boat like *Ellen Marie* did in my painting.

Dave and I continued to share treasures of information, such as who had owned and built a model of *Ellen Marie*'s sister ship, *Moby Dick.* When Jen Shepley and I visited the Euro Ship Store in Fairhaven to meet Sonja Sovik and look for photos of *Ellen Marie,* we had followed Sonja out to the street so she could point to Reidar Bendiksen's fishing-gear shop. Sonja believed that Reidar had built a model of *Ellen Marie,* but I learned when I visited Reidar that he had constructed a miniature of his vessel, *Moby Dick.*

This was the information from Dave's data sheet for *Ellen Marie:*

Vessel Name:	Ellen Marie
Builder's Hull #:	217
Date Launched:	2/11/1961
Vessel Type:	Dragger
Original Use:	Fishing
Length:	80
Hull Material:	Wood
Builder:	Gamage, Harvey F.
Designer:	Simpson, Dwight S.
Original Owner:	Joseph Perry
Owner Location:	New Bedford, MA

Sea Trial, courtesy of South Bristol Historical Society

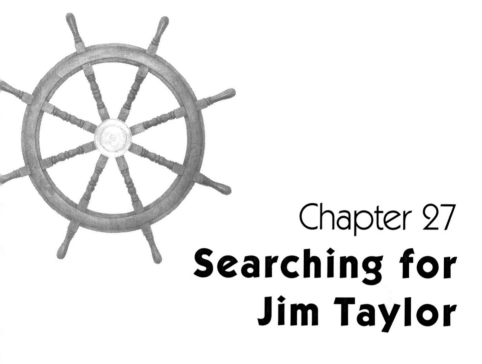

Chapter 27
Searching for Jim Taylor

To find *Ellen Marie*'s third owner, James S. Taylor, I leaned heavily on the Coast Guard title information. There was an endorsement port listed for the entry of each purchase. Most were New Bedford. Taylor's was Plymouth. I felt fairly confident that the James S. Taylor whom I'd located on the Internet was the right one for two reasons: a connection to a fishing business and his location—one of his two addresses was in Sandwich, Massachusetts, across the Cape Cod Canal but otherwise adjacent to Plymouth. The other address was in Florida. I dialed the only phone number listed under his name, which was associated with the Florida address, and prepared to take copious notes on an informative conversation. When a woman answered the phone, I asked if she was Mrs. Taylor. She was, so I introduced myself and asked, "Did your husband ever own the *Ellen Marie?*"

"No. Never heard of it," she replied.

It took me a few seconds to recover from the surprise before I could force a polite "Thank you anyway. Have a nice day."

There was a bigger surprise at my Friday morning Dunkin' Donuts coffee klatch. Rosemary McDevitt asked what book our friend Jeannie was looking at. Jeannie held up my copy of *The Dragger* and said, "Rachel's doing research on this boat."

Rosemary didn't respond to that, but she shared that she had worked in the fishing industry for years in Boston. She had done boat settlements, which meant that she had paid the fishermen their portion of the net profit of the catch.

The following Friday, on the way out of the coffee shop, Rosemary asked me how my research was going.

"I'm trying to find one of *Ellen Marie*'s owners," I said, "but I'm not having much luck."

She asked who it was.

"His name is James S. Taylor."

"Jimmy Taylor? I bought a house from him," Rosemary said as if it should have been no big surprise.

"What? You've got to be kidding," I said, flabbergasted.

"No. Really. Call me later."

When I called her, Rosemary was trying to find papers for the house she had bought from Jimmy Taylor in Sandwich. She talked while she searched. "I worked for F. J. O'Hara & Sons doing boat settlements," she explained. "The fishermen always treated me with respect. They taught me how to tie ropes and told me stories about ghosts. They're real superstitious. There's lots you can't do, like back into a sunset. The government has killed the fishing industry for these guys," she declared, referring to big Russian trawlers, pollution, and regulations.

She continued, "They used to tell me, 'Don't let him'—meaning my husband—'don't let him go fishing, because once he gets it in his blood, that's all he'll want to do.' It's true. He fished in New Bedford in the '70s."

Her husband entered the room then, and Rosemary asked him, "Didn't Jimmy Taylor own the *Ellen Marie*?"

I could hear his response: "The *Ellen Marie*? Yuh. She was a scalloper. Bought her in the scalloping boom."

Rosemary asked, "He died, didn't he?"

"About ten years ago," he confirmed.

Rosemary's attention turned back to me on the phone. "The house was on Pine Street near Heritage Plantation. It had fishing-boat-yellow trim." I pictured a color as bright as a yellow slicker.

Days later, I looked back in my notes to check the Sandwich, Massachusetts, address I'd taken from the Internet search when I had been so sure I had found the right James Taylor. It was Pine Street. I made a mental note of the Pine Street house number and asked Rosemary the next time I saw her if it had been her address. The answer was yes.

Chapter 28
The Cook

On October 28, I took my copy of *The Dragger* to share it with Edward Patenaude, the cook on *Ellen Marie* when the book's author had been aboard. We sat side by side on a sofa in his home in Fairhaven while his daughter put Mrs. Patenaude's hair in rollers near the kitchen sink.

"I know this lumper," he said, poking the first picture he saw on page 127. "They take over. They unload the ship." Mr. Patenaude spoke in present tense as if he was living the experience when, in fact, thirty-five years had elapsed since he had been part of *Ellen Marie*'s crew.

We flipped to the front of the book, where his attention went to *Ellen Marie*'s dory in the picture that had made her come alive to me when I saw it at the Middleboro Library four weeks earlier. He said it was near impossible to set out the lifeboat in a storm. "All you got left is a life preserver," he said. "They came out with a new suit. You had to tell the storm, 'Hold on while I get into the suit.' You're rolling all over the deck. Water's coming in from the scup holes."

A mean storm couldn't respect that scuppers, the holes in the vessel's sidewalls at deck level, had been designed to drain the sea *out*, not let it in. "Everything had to be latched down," he said. "It can come when you're asleep. When it changes out there, you have to be ready."

We turned to a picture of Captain Bowers and two crew members sitting at the table in the forecastle—the living quarters. The captain, gazing at the stew pot and looking pensive, leaned both forearms on the upturned table edge. He was a dark-haired man with a mole on his right cheek.

The former cook described his old working area: "Under the seats—that's where you store the groceries. The table sides flip down. When you have hard weather—you can have hard weather for three days—the ridge and that rim on the table keep the plates from sliding. The bow and the bunks are forward. The refrigerator was over here"—he pointed behind him to the left—"then the sink and the stove over here." He pointed behind him to the right. "You had to pump water just like on a farm."

We loitered over a wheelhouse photo. The camera had been close to the spaced slat flooring, directed up to the ship's wheel and the simple pipe-and-disk seat that stood before it. A pair of turned-down thigh-high rubber boots, one on its side, had been left on the slatted floor between the austere seat and the wheel. There was nothing but white beyond the two main wheelhouse windows. Mr. Patenaude explained that Captain Bowers's stateroom with all his maps was behind where the photographer must have been to take the picture. Perhaps the white beyond the windows inspired his comment, "When you go out there, you got fog all the time—mist in the winter."

He referred to Captain Bowers as "quite a guy" from Nova Scotia. "He was a good captain," he said, "and a strict Catholic. When he wasn't getting in fish, he'd say, 'Curse of the Lord Jesus on you.' When anything happened, he'd say, 'Why do you do this to me?' His arms would be up in the air. I got along good with him. I used to feel funny when he'd curse at God … talk to him just like he was on deck. They'd pray the rosary every night," Mr. Patenaude said of the other crew members and the captain. Mr. Patenaude wasn't a Catholic.

"We always had meetings and Christmas parties," he said. "Now they use less men. They're more mechanized."

Mr. Patenaude interrupted his thoughts about modern fishing when we turned to a close-up of a dripping net full of flatfish. "There's a chain," he said, "in the bottom of the net with rubber tires to preserve the chain and keep it from getting held up on rocks."

He said that they dropped the net when the bottom of it cleared the deck plate, but I didn't know what a deck plate was, and I foolishly didn't ask. During the fishing process, the speed of the boat had to be controlled in the wheelhouse, and two men had to operate the two winch wheels to let out the net. "The captain," he said, "rings the bell and yells starboard or port depending which side he wants the net dropped. They would get tangled if they were set out together. There are all kinds of signals."

We turned to a page to see a brawny man in boots, oilers, t-shirt, and cap gutting a fish. "That's me!" he said with surprise. He described the gutting process. On the opposite page, a man in a plaid shirt, boots, and bib oilers stood knee-deep in fish, pitching them into the hold.

I could picture what he described next. When the bell rang to signal the raising of the net, gears churned, the cables went taut, and seagulls attacked the net even before it had broken the surface of the water. As obedient to the bell as Pavlov's dogs, gulls picked at the eyes of the fish as the net was raised. It looked like the haul was a catch of seagulls.

Mr. Patenaude remembered the trips ending at the Cultivator Club, a private place across from Ship Supply near the New Bedford waterfront. I wished I could have been one of the gang, but I knew that I didn't even begin to have the credentials to walk through the door where some of the most courageous fishermen enjoyed camaraderie and tipped a few in celebration.

I was oblivious to the amount of time we were spending in review of *The Dragger* until I sensed that Mrs. Patenaude, who had taken a seat in the room, seemed anxious for her husband to have a break. She glanced at him more than once as if she was concerned for his well-being. Overstaying would have spoiled the goal of giving Mr. Patenaude the joy of reliving his *Ellen Marie* experience, so I thanked them for allowing me to visit and went on my way.

Chapter 29
Off Course

Steve Kennedy, the Cape photographer whose photos were sold at the Ship Store where I met Sonja Sovik, made a surprising statement about *Ellen Marie*'s crew. "There's a woman on the Cape who was scalloping on the boat," he said. "Her name is Rosalie Nadeau. She's an artist ... shows her paintings the same place I do—at the Left Bank Gallery."

Trying to picture a female artist as a scalloper challenged my stereotypic thinking that a fisherman had to be brawny and tough. "Do you know how I can get in touch with her?" I asked. He gave me her telephone number, and I reached her in mid-November.

Rosalie was more than willing to reminisce about her experience on the boat, even referring to photographs she could share. But it wasn't a convenient time to chat; she was busy preparing for a trip south. She gave me her e-mail address and suggested that we get together sometime in January, cautioning that the passage of thirty years might have limited her memories.

Two things that Rosalie said didn't dovetail with what I already knew. The boat she'd fished had docked in Provincetown, and its captain had been Bud Doyle. She remembered fishing in 1976, but I understood that Captain Bowers had *Ellen Marie* until 1978. Who was Bud Doyle, and why would he have moved the boat out of New Bedford?"

"You know, Rosalie," I said, "I'm not sure that we are talking about the same boat. Do you know who owned her?" She didn't; nor did she know how to reach Bud Doyle, where he lived, or his real first name. I wanted to ask him who had owned the boat when he'd been skipper. If it wasn't one of the owners on *Ellen Marie*'s title, then Rosalie had fished on a different boat. Rosalie said that she would look through some files when she returned from Florida to help locate Captain Bud Doyle.

I didn't have the patience to wait for her return. I went to my Nadeau file to see if I had the last name of the person who'd told Rosalie that *Ellen Marie* had been sold to Jimmy Taylor. His first name was Luther. I'd hoped he could direct me to Bud Doyle, but my notes didn't help. So I tried the Internet white pages and found a name, address, and phone number of a Mr. Doyle in Orleans. Since that was the Cape Cod town where Rosalie lived, I reasoned it might be Captain Bud. I printed the information.

What was there to lose? I called the man, introduced myself, and told him about my goal to find *Ellen Marie*. "By any chance," I asked, "are you the Bud Doyle that was her skipper in 1976?"

He wasn't. But like so many others I had met on my adventure, he didn't dismiss me quickly. He did his best to help find the right Bud Doyle. "Hold on, let me see," he said, putting the phone down to look for his phone book. Such a long time passed that I wondered if he'd forgotten that he had a pending call until I heard the scuff of slippered feet approaching. He explained that he had had to find his glasses. While he carefully and *slowly* perused all the Doyles in the Cape Cod phone book, I relaxed into total acceptance and doodled TWBD (thy will be done) and an arrow on the paper next to his name and phone number. No listing seemed to be the one he hoped to find for the man he said used to run the *Globe* distribution—Larry Doyle from Brewster, a neighboring town.

I asked if he knew anyone in the fishing industry who might possibly know Bud Doyle. "Ken Collins," he said. "He used to be a trade teacher at Nauset Regional. He knows just about everything." Mr. Doyle began another slow and careful phonebook search, this time for Mr. Collins. I retraced and added a couple of lines to the arrow doodle while I waited, full of gratitude and acceptance, totally at ease, and feeling spiritually connected to the stranger on the other end of the phone. He gave me the name and number of Ken Collins in Eastham, after which I expressed sincere gratitude for his kindness.

Moments later, I told Mr. Collins that I had gotten his phone number from Mr. Doyle. Mr. Collins seemed primed for a conversation about fishing vessels. Without hesitation, he responded to my introduction by saying, "I'm looking at the *Cape Ann* right now from 1948. She had six thousand pounds of scallops on board when she wrecked. I've got the engine-room gong. I went over a steep bank to get to her—went down to the engine room. The sea hit the stern three times. Three times I went up to see if the water had come up around the bow."

"What are you looking at," I asked, confused. "A picture? A model?"

He said it was a painting. When he asked how I happened to reach his good friend Joe Doyle, I told him about Rosalie Nadeau scalloping on *Ellen Marie* when Bud Doyle was captain, and I told him why I wanted to reach Bud Doyle. He didn't know Captain Doyle or have any suggestions on how to reach him.

"There's a well-known artist down here named Nadeau who does ceramic flounders," he said. I made a mental note to check with Rosalie about that and asked Mr. Collins if he'd been a commercial fisherman.

"No. I was a marine engineer on the *Constitution*, the American Export line."

I told him a story that Rudy Matland, son of *Ellen Marie*'s second owner, had told me the day before about fishing on the *Rush*, a boat his father had owned before *Ellen Marie*. Rudy had been on the rear deck. The fog had been thick, and whistles had been blowing. Out of the fog, a ship that seemed "as tall as the Empire State Building" had come alongside. It had turned out to be the *Stockholm*. Mr. Matland had said, "It scared the devil out of me."

When Mr. Matland told me that story, it took some time to remember why the name *Stockholm* seemed familiar. When I was twelve, the *Stockholm* hit the *Andrea Doria*'s midsection off the coast of Massachusetts. I remembered seeing film of *Andrea Doria* sinking on TV.

Mr. Collins recognized the *Stockholm* immediately and said, "The

Andrea Doria was a duplicate of the *Constitution*." He apologized for not knowing Bud Doyle, adding, "I like talking to people like you."

"My pleasure," I said, and I meant it.

Rosalie confirmed that she was the artist who created the ceramic flounders. In December she wrote again, embarrassed that she had been confused. One of her former shipmates had informed her that their boat was called *Kathryn Marie*, not *Ellen Marie*. She wished me luck in my endeavor and added that it had been fun talking with me and trying to remember old times.

Not long after, the tall, dark-haired Rosalie who had fished for scallops on *Kathryn Marie* invited me to visit. In her light, spacious backyard studio, where her magnificent oil and pastel fishing scenes and still lifes surrounded us, Rosalie shared pictures of her experience on the boat. Later, in her basement workshop, I sat on a high stool near long, dusty tables covered with not-yet-fired gray clay flounders and lemon sole and watched Rosalie detail gills and eyes. I purchased a flounder and two shiny blue lemon sole platters and hung them on my living-room wall over the terra-cotta chair that had been inspired by *The Pilot House*.

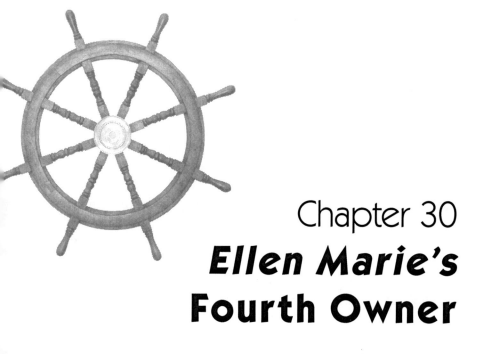

Chapter 30
Ellen Marie's
Fourth Owner

Steve Kennedy, the Cape photographer, had left some pictures of *Ellen Marie* for me at the Ship Store in Fairhaven. The day I bought them, I explained to Sonja Sovik that *Ellen Marie's* title listed Boat Ellen Marie Inc. as the first and fourth owners. I told her that the corporation's address had been 2 Middle Street, Fairhaven, and asked her if she knew who the principals might have been.

Just as I suspected, Sonja was able to usher me to the answer. She led me out of the shop, around the street corner, and through a door of the same building to Solveig's. She introduced me to Marjorie Orman, whose business was boat settlements—that is, distribution of catch profit to the crew. I explained the mystery to Marjorie. "When I had her," she said (meaning *Ellen Marie* for boat settlement), "she was owned by Donald Calnan. Donald Calnan is Boat Ellen Marie." She found Mr. Calnan's address and telephone number and gave it to me.

There were many unsuccessful attempts to reach Mr. Calnan by phone. One day, on a whim, I dialed the number and, just as I had many times before, listened to it ring and ring, expecting no one to answer.

A woman's hello took me by surprise. Bernice Calnan said that she and Mr. Calnan had just returned from a trip to Florida.

I asked Mr. Calnan if he had been one of the incorporators of Boat Ellen Marie Inc. with Mr. Perry. The answer was no. *Ellen Marie*'s fourth owner, Boat Ellen Marie Inc., was not a revitalization of Mr. Perry's corporation at all. It had been a brand-new corporation. Mr. Calnan reminded me that when a corporation was dissolved as Mr. Perry's had been, the name could be used again. I judged myself harshly for not realizing that. He had purchased *Ellen Marie* in partnership with a man named Richard Flood.

Ellen Marie was a scalloper the entire time that Mr. Calnan owned her. He said, "There were four specific jobs: the cook, the mate, the engineer, and the skipper. The crew did the work—operated the gear and cut the scallops. She was a good sea boat."

"Why did you sell her?" I asked.

"The boat was getting old," he said, "and I was improving myself." I assumed he meant that he had pursued a steel vessel the way others had done.

Sometime later, I looked again at the corporation papers I had printed and the list of businesses I had found on the Internet for 2 Middle Street, the office address of Boat Ellen Marie Inc. There it was in black and white: "Éuro Ship Store, 2 Middle Street, Fairhaven." Why had I not recognized it before? Although I had suspected that Sonja could help me, the puzzle pieces hadn't fit together in my head that the store and the corporation shared the same address.

Chapter 31
Bind Us Together, Lord

While enjoying lunch at a corner table at The Little Phoenix, a restaurant in the Sassaquin section of New Bedford, I was startled by television news that I thought I might have misheard. I asked Cali, the waitress who was standing at the end of the counter, "Did a New Bedford fishing boat go down?"

"Yuh," Cali responded. "The *Lady of Grace*. Four fishermen are missing."

I was deeply saddened. I had bonded with the fishing community through *Ellen Marie*. I wanted to reach out, but I didn't know how. Certainly the loss of the *Lady of Grace* and her crew would have caused Shelly at the Harbor Commission to relive the loss of her dad. I took a box of donuts to Shelly at her office. It was the only thing I could think of to show I cared. As if compelled, I followed the tragedy through the newspaper for days.

The Friday before Valentine's Day, I attended a fundraiser in New Bedford for the Fishermen's Tribute Fund, the goal of which was to create a monument to all within the fishing industry, especially those who lost their lives. The plan was to erect the monument at Fort Taber, a peninsula bounded by New Bedford Harbor and Buzzards Bay, where the expression of love would be the last thing fishermen saw when they left New Bedford and the first thing they saw when they returned. I didn't know until Shelly told me late in the evening that the first person I met that night, Anna, was the mother of Mike Viera, who had died with Shelly's father, Karl Schlemmer, when the *Wanderer* capsized in 1994.

I went to Anna at the end of the evening to say how sorry I was that she had experienced the tragic loss of her son. She told me that losing him had created a void impossible to fill—a void that no one could understand.

"You may think I'm crazy," she said, "but I get comfort from knowing that they were tied together. He wasn't alone."

"You mean they were literally tied together?"

"Yes," she said. "With a rope."

Anna's words floated to consciousness days later as I puttered around the house and hummed a familiar chorus. Surprised by the connection between her son's experience and the lyrics, I sat still and allowed the sadness of the losses of the *Wanderer*, the *Lady of Grace,* and others to wash over me as I sang:

> Bind us together, Lord.
> Bind us together
> With cords that cannot be broken;
> Bind us together, Lord.
> Bind us together with love.

How I wished that I could tell the whole fishing community that I cared—that God cared. I thought about that for a moment—those words: "He cares for you." *Aren't they in the Bible?* I did some research. I found them, and they were written by Peter, a fisherman! "Humble yourselves, therefore, under God's mighty hand, that he may lift you up in due time. Cast all your anxiety on him because he cares for you" (1 Peter 5:6).

Chapter 32
The Convoy

It was January 27, 2007. For hours leading up to meeting Captain Bowers in person, I was both excited and anxious. To avoid making a negative impression, I manipulated the timing of my arrival at his daughter and son-in-law's house in South Dartmouth by driving beyond, past clapboard-front colonials, shingled capes, and stone walls, to Padanaram Bridge. The short, shallow-arched bridge and its low, easily flooded road extension that crossed Apponagansett Bay led to a boat-launching area, stark in its winter emptiness, where I reversed direction. I rang the doorbell of the white house at precisely the appointed time of three o'clock. Captain Bowers and his daughter, Susan, greeted me at the door. I followed *Ellen Marie*'s first captain, not quite as tall and dark as he seemed in pictures in *The Dragger*, down a narrow hallway to the pristine white kitchen where we sat next to each other on stools at the room's center island. As Susan poured coffee, Captain Bowers wasted no time on introductory chitchat but immediately talked of fishing with *Ellen Marie* on Georges Bank.

"A convoy was sunk," he began, his tenor-range voice as rough as sandpaper, "and we didn't know about it until later years, and then I found out about it. I got it pretty well pinpointed." He rounded the *r* in *years*, his Nova Scotian accent contrasting to the native *ye-uhs*.

"A convoy?" I was drawing a blank. I knew I had heard the word and that I should know, but for whatever reason, I couldn't remember what a convoy was.

"Yuh," he said. "A convoy. You know—they used to sail through the war years, and the Germans used to lay in wait for 'em. Submarines would sink the ships. A lot of them was right on the fishing grounds—especially one convoy. I don't know how many ships was sunk right in one of the best fishing areas. But I got that all worked out so that we kept clear of it." With rising intonation, he added, "But we used to go as close as we could."

I wondered if it was imp, daredevil, or covetous fisherman who tempted fate. It reminded me of my childhood at the family camp on Sampson's Pond in Carver, Massachusetts. I felt compelled on occasion to row out to the place where there was a gigantic dark boulder under water or the place where there was a sunken boat. I knew that when I saw the submerged objects it would feel as if my stomach turned upside down. I never understood why that happened or why I felt drawn to do it. I had reacted with a related fear when I imagined storm waters rising over the Padanaram Bridge road.

Captain Bowers went on. "One place later on I was getting big fish, and I got a little too close and I hooked one of the wrecks."

"Did you lose your net?" I asked.

"No, I got the net back, but it was all tore to pieces."

I had a feeling that there was more to that story, but Susan drew our attention to a package she was about to open.

Chapter 33
Launching Photos

Eight-by-ten-inch photographs spilled out of the brown envelope onto the island counter. Susan said, "These are some pictures that weren't put in *The Dragger*. I've never seen them. My father had them stashed away."

"Oh, wow!" I exclaimed, excited as a child. Most but not all of the photos had been taken by Finn, *The Dragger* author.

Captain Bowers began to explain one of the photos. "That's the vessel. That's on the railway when she—"

"The Launching photos!" I interrupted with glee. I had given up hope of ever seeing *Ellen Marie*'s launching photos after I learned that David Andrews, the South Bristol Gamage boat historian, had none.

"That's South Bristol, Maine—Gamage's Yard," explained the captain.

In the photo, *Ellen Marie*'s shiny dark hull towered over the men who were standing near the closed bay doors through which she would be born on that cold February day in 1961. A woman, a boy, and a girl, bundled in winter garb, waited for the launching. One child wore a striped scarf, the other a fur-trimmed hooded coat, and 1960s-style crocheted ear warmers covered the woman's ears. Snow littered the shoulders of her dark cloth coat.

I flipped pages in my loose-leaf notebook, looking for a picture of the big gray shed to show Captain Bowers, Susan, and her husband, Rody (short for Roderick but pronounced with a long *o*), but I hadn't brought one.

Rody asked if the Gamage Yard still built boats.

"No," I answered. "As a matter of fact, they're tearing the shed down," I said, irresponsibly passing on what I had heard in South Bristol. I lifted a photograph for them to see. "That's a picture of my painting. That's *The Pilot House.*"

We refocused on the launching photos. A woman wearing a luxurious dark fur coat and hat held a ribbon-wrapped christening bottle and grinned for the camera. We wondered who she was. Susan, thinking that the photographer might know, read the photographer's stamp on the back of the photo: "Pictorial Studio, Newcastle, Maine—1961."

"That's probably Ivan Flye," I said. I explained that I had spoken with Edward Gamage, Harvey Gamage's nephew, and his wife, Bunny, on the phone in November. They had mentioned Mr. Flye when I asked who might have taken launching pictures, but the photographer had passed away.

"Now, Dad," Susan asked, "you weren't there when she was christened, were you?"

"No," he said. "She was launched when I got up there. She was in the water then. When we went up, she was supposed to be ready for us to bring her to New Bedford."

I stared at the most sensational photo of my *Ellen Marie* framed in the open bay doorway of the big gray shed. Her cradle had slid down the rails, disturbing the icy waters in which her virgin hull was about to be baptized. The ribbons that wrapped the christening bottle, dangling from a line attached to her bow, hung low by the nose of her keel, and a capped man on her bow appeared to hold a rope that crossed like a raised eyebrow above her port-side name. They were sliding into fog and snow.

Ellen Marie's screw – taken by Ivan Flye

Ready for christening – taken by Ivan Flye

Ellen Marie's launching at the Harvey Gamage
Shipyard taken by Ivan Flye

Ellen Marie's launching at the Harvey Gamage
Shipyard taken by Ivan Flye

Chapter 34
Something's Different about Her

In the early stages of my adventure, I feared more than once that I might have been mixing up two boats named *Ellen Marie*. The dory difference was one reason. When I saw *Ellen Marie*'s sea-trial photo, which I received from Dave Andrews, I noticed that there were two covered dories on her. There was only one dory, without a cover, in *The Pilot House*. I mentioned the dories to Captain Bowers.

"They was there all through the time I had her," he said. "I took good care of those dories, because if anything ever happened, that's all you had for the crew to get off in."

The lifeboats triggered special memories for Captain Bowers's daughter, Susan. "I remember as kids," she said, "we used to take a ferry over to the Vineyard. He'd unload there, and we'd ride back in the dories."

"What a thrill that must have been," I said with a tinge of jealousy.

I asked if they knew when *Ellen Marie* began carrying just one boat. Captain Bowers didn't know. "That must have been after Matland sold the boat and the other fellas got her," he said.

I told them that Dave Andrews had suggested a change in Coast

Guard rules as an explanation and that he had noted that Gamage boats of the 1970s carried only one dory. I put to rest any concern based on the number of lifeboats that I might have confused more than one *Ellen Marie.*

Captain Bowers had his own story about change. It began shortly after *Ellen Marie* arrived in New Bedford. He said, "I had the forecastle all rigged up. I put a refrigerator in there and hot and cold water and a special sink for the men washing and shaving. I put all that stuff in. It was the only boat in New Bedford that had that. I did it myself. And it was such a trivial cost. It was so small to be done, you know, but it was so beneficial for the crew. People come aboard, they classed her as a yacht. That's the way we kept her up for seventeen years."

He sounded sad when he told me that *Ellen Marie*'s condition had gone downhill after Mr. Matland sold her. "The forecastle," he said, dropping his left hand, "oh, what a mess." But he perked up to say, "I never missed a trip for seventeen years on that boat. That's a long time. Quite a jail sentence, huh?"

"I guess so." I smiled. I admired his pride in his boat and his care for his crew.

A design difference had caused confusion ever since Steve Kennedy gave me the photo of *Ellen Marie* as the *Three Vs.* The stern configuration bothered me until Captain Bowers and I came to a photo of the stern of *Ellen Marie* when she was new. Pointing to what I thought was rear deck behind the wheelhouse, I asked, "Could you walk behind here? Was that area open so that you could walk behind there?"

"Yuh," he answered. "You could. It was very narrow ..."

Turning to Steve Kennedy's photo of the *Three Vs*, I pointed to the wheelhouse extension that eliminated a walkway. Rody, a fisherman himself, understood my confusion and explained, "Scallop boats are different. They enclose it."

I asked him for what purpose.

"On a dragger they do all the work on deck," Rody said. "On a scallop boat, you take all the scallops off the deck, bring them back here where we open them. They enclose it all the way around so we're protected."

"If it wasn't for the numbers," I said, "I would have wondered if the *Three Vs* was a different boat with the stern built in the way it was."

I thought back to the federal buyback of groundfish draggers when boat owners had had to destroy or change the use of their vessels. For some reason, at the beginning of my search for *Ellen Marie*, even though I had read that changing the use of a vessel was an option, I had blocked that option from consideration. It was so simple. *Ellen Marie* hadn't been taken by the buyback program because she was no longer a groundfish dragger! When I had spoken with David Osier in September, I had assured him emphatically that *Ellen Marie* was a groundfish dragger, not a scalloper. Truth was that before the federal buyback program, after Captain Bowers's seventeen years, *Ellen Marie* had been converted to scalloping. It was both ego deflating and amusing to retrospectively observe, in the light of the facts, how sure I had been about what I had thought and said.

Steve Kennedy photo

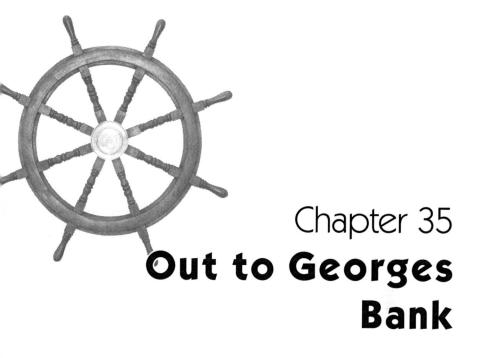

Chapter 35
Out to Georges Bank

Captain Bowers had agreed to take his daughter, Susan, and me fishing in our imaginations aboard *Ellen Marie*.

"The first thing," he explained, "when you're getting ready on a fishing trip, you have the date you're sailing—the day you're supposed to go out, the day you set sail."

"You decide that. Right?"

He looked up as if distracted. "Yuh," he said and continued. "Say we're supposed to go out on Thursday," the captain said. "The first thing in the morning, my job is to get the boat in to the ice pier. Usually seven or eight o'clock, I have the boat right under the ice chute. And I have a lumper who puts the ice in the pen. This chute comes down, fills all the pens. They know how to do it. Then I don't have to bother. Once the boat is there, the hatch comes off. The lumper takes care of icing the boat down. The fuel—that's all taken care of by whatever oil company takes care of us. When the boat comes into the pier, they come aboard. They fill the tanks."

"What pier would we be at?" I asked.

"Pier 3. That usually was our pier where we used to tie up."

"Does the pier have a name now?" I asked. "Is it near Steamship Pier?"

"It's still pier 3," Susan explained. "It's where the visitors center is now. That's pier 3. Years ago, when you pulled into the dock you had a restaurant—Jimmy C's, a little place, but it doesn't look like it did years ago."

"Pier 3 was mostly draggers at that time," he said, refocusing on our fishing trip. He explained that after the ice and fuel were aboard, New Bedford Ship Supply or whatever outfit the cook had given his order to would bring a truck down and put the supplies into the forecastle. The meats they put in the refrigerator; the rest the cook stowed away.

I asked how long we would be out.

"Usually we figure a week—six, seven days. Sometimes if we hit fish, a lot of fish, maybe five days. According to what we catch. Sometimes we go two, three days and don't find fish at all. Then maybe we fish eight days. Usually the run is from five to eight days. Once you got all your supplies aboard, well then, around eleven o'clock you call sailing time. Then everybody's aboard."

"You use the same crew all the time?"

"Sometimes for years the same crew. Once in a while one fella will change around. Sometimes they go away then after a while they come back again."

"Are we heading out now?" I asked.

"We're going out across Buzzards Bay," the captain said in a slow rhythm that suggested the movement of the boat.

"Wait. You forgot to put the radar on," Sue chided in jest, making us laugh.

"Oh, don't bother," her father said. "Them times radar wasn't very good—when *Ellen Marie* was new. There was very poor reception. But anyway, we'd go out Buzzards Bay across Woods Hole, through Woods Hole, then down the Sound."

"Nantucket Sound?" I asked, hoping to know at least something.

"Nantucket Sound," he confirmed and continued in the boat's rhythm. "Across the rip down to Great Point, Great Round Shoal Channel ... get out to Great Round Shoal Channel, then you set the course. Usually, we went offshore to what we call Georges. You'd be all night. Time you got through Round Shoal Channel, it would be practically dark then. By morning you'd be down to the fishing grounds on Georges Bank."

"So it took about a day to get there," I said.

"Oh yuh. You figure it would be over a hundred miles to where we're going out to Georges Bank. We'd go out to what we call the eastern part of Georges Bank. That's where you used to get the lemon sole. You had to go out there to get them and the haddock. Codfish—you could get the codfish right on Nantucket Shoals. But you couldn't make a trip on codfish alone, because they didn't want all codfish. All right if you had a small amount. You'd get a fair price for them, but you couldn't bring a whole boatload of 'em. You could go to Nantucket Shoals and load the boat with cod, but you wouldn't get nothin' for it. You're working for nothin'."

I was impressed by his business acumen.

"The other boats couldn't keep up with us, because, number one, they didn't have the boats to go out there in that kind of weather you get sometimes."

Sue laid a chart on the counter and said, "That gives you an idea of where you're going on your trip."

I located Nantucket Shoals and the Great South Channel.

Captain Bowers pointed to light blue finger shapes running in a northerly to southerly direction on a sea of white. Black depth notations, most double, some single digits, looked like a swarm of gnats. "This is shoal water in here," he said. "If there was any kind of a sea, this breaks. The sea breaks here. Boats can't go across here—the shoals."

"What does that mean?" I asked. "That it's all rocky?"

"Big sandbars," the captain explained.

"Very shallow," Sue added.

"Maybe fifteen or twenty miles across this area," her father continued with a sweep of his hand. "But you can come down between if you know your way. I used to have my loran bearings, and I could come down between the rips. If you watched, you could see the rips in the water. See the water boiling. Stay between them. But you got to be careful. Once you get clear of this one, out through here you could go. In through these areas here—great places for fish in through here." He pointed east of the shoals. "See, the other boats could never go down there."

"Because of the rips?" I wondered.

"Well, I don't know. They just didn't seem to have the boats them times. Like the *Ellen Marie* was a new boat. I could go anywheres with that boat. She was new."

"How much would she draw?" Sue asked.

"I think it was nine feet. That was just normal. When she was loaded, possibly eleven."

I still wanted to understand why *Ellen Marie* could do things that other boats couldn't, so I asked if it was because *Ellen Marie* was so much bigger than the other boats. "Well, fairly bigger," the captain answered, "but see, she was new and strong. A lot of them boats ... I don't know. They had new ones built, but they wasn't built like the *Ellen Marie*. They didn't seem to have the stuff like *Ellen Marie* had as far as seaworthiness."

"Harvey Gamage knew what he was doing, huh?"

"Oh yeah," the captain agreed. "He could build a good boat. See, a lot of them boats ... I don't know why, but nobody ever followed us. You'd never see any other boats. The only boats that we'd see around would be maybe somebody from Gloucester or somethin'—them Gloucester boats once in a while. But they wouldn't come in on the shoals either, because they looked for different species of fish. See, they were looking for cod-fish and haddock. Gloucester didn't want flat fish. Another species they wanted was red fish."

"Who was the market that wanted the—"

Before I could say "flat fish," Captain Bowers responded, "New York. New York wanted the flounder. These buyers—Tishcon was one of the big ones and Ell Vee Dee."

I thought about *Ellen Marie*'s isolation in the good fishing area. Was it because *Ellen Marie* was built special, or was it her captain? I con-cluded that one could not have excelled in the best fishing areas without the other. I believed that Captain Bowers's unclear explanation of why other boats did not fish where he took *Ellen Marie* was an indication of his humility, his work ethic, his ability to handle a good boat, and his courage to take reasonable risks. Another story supported my conclusion.

"This is what you call big yellowtails and lemon sole," he said,

pointing to a netted catch photo in *The Dragger*. We'd go in there and
load the boat and have her full—all the pens full of fish—and they'd
say, 'Where'd you get those?' When the buyers would see these fish, they
were number-one quality, and of course we'd go to that area and work.
They were scared of the wrecks. I didn't give a damn about the wrecks.
What if we did lose a net? What we were taking in would pay for the nets
over and over. I had to mend the nets, put the nets together myself. I was
working twine in the pilot house while we were towing—still making up
sections of nets all the time. Steady. Making up. Always had spare stuff
ready. If we lost something, we'd have parts under the whaleback ready."

I knew that the whaleback was a storage area in the bow. His train
of thought switched to his crew. He said, "I had men from New York,
Gloucester, Boston, all over. Of course I worked them hard."

We chuckled.

"They didn't get away easy," he admitted.

Susan added, "If you were to ask anybody back then about my dad,
they'd say, 'Oh yuh, that Woodie Bowers—he was tough. Oh yes.'"

"We brought the fish," he said with a hint of a grin. "We brought
the money."

That was all we needed to know.

Visitors Center, New Bedford Ship Supply
Co., dome of the Whaling Museum

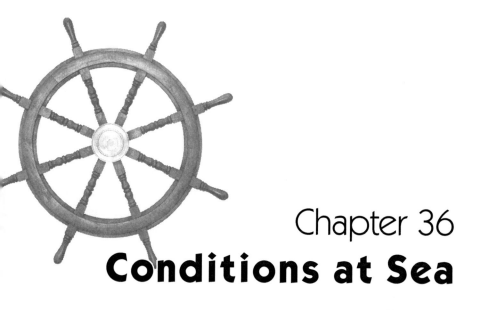

Chapter 36
Conditions at Sea

While on our imaginary trip to Georges Bank, Captain Bowers reminisced about Bill Finn's actual trips.

"*Ellen Marie*—we had plenty of room to take another man, so I said, 'Sure. Bring him aboard,'" Bowers said, referring to Finn. "So I told him, 'You understand, now, that we go out a week.' He said, 'All right.' He got sick the first couple days, and I used to talk to him. 'Now get a cigarette. Start smoking. Get up here in the pilot house and talk to me.' He was a wonderful man. He forgot about that he was seasick. Then he started climbing up the mast with his cameras, and he was all over everywheres taking pictures."

I asked if Captain Bowers had been nervous when Finn started climbing masts. He said he'd been more concerned about the photographer's seasickness. He explained that Finn used a sling so his hands were free and a strap that he put around the rigging. Once the captain was satisfied that Finn felt better and he knew how Finn had prepared for his own safety, he was no longer worried.

Captain Bowers smiled an impish grin. "This fellow here, you know … we were out there one day. It was blowing a gale—blowing hard. Finn said, 'How far are we from land?' I said, 'We're half a mile from land.' He said, 'A half a mile? I can't see land.' 'You ain't looking the right way, I said. 'It's this way—down.'" The captain's grin widened as he pumped his pointing finger up and down, referring to the ocean floor.

A moment later, he sighed and said, "There was times when I used to get tired, you know, jogging out these gales. What the hell are you going to do? You're out there. You can't get to Nantucket, where you could lay smooth. Once you're out there, across the channel on Georges' side, you gotta suffer it out. You know—stay in the lee of the rips if you can, but then to do that you've got to be joggin' up all the time. It's worse than fishing. Fishing—you don't seem to mind it, but when you're joggin' like that in a gale of wind, ah, God. Time goes so godly slow. Then suppose you get a blow for three days?"

I sympathized, saying that it must have worn him out physically and mentally. If I had actually been on *Ellen Marie* in a gale, I would have been afraid and would have wanted to go home, but I kept those thoughts to myself.

"Yuh," he agreed. You're wore out just waiting for the time to come that it gets fit to go fishing. Then you don't feel like working."

What was it about these tales of the sea that captivated me so? The second time we had had a phone conversation, I had listened like a child at a storyteller's feet as he told about bringing *Ellen Marie* home to New Bedford. Now, still mesmerized, I soaked up these stories like a sponge.

Captain Bowers, praising Finn's ability to capture a story on film, flipped open a copy of *The Dragger* lying on the counter and stopped at a close-up photo of himself in the pilot house. The brim of his black captain's cap glistened above his thick black eyebrows. I could almost feel the texture of the upturned collar of his black wool outer shirt, the heavy brushed cotton shoulder strap to his oilers, the rough stubble on his cheek and chin, and the short hairs of his mustache. I imagined the smell of the cigarette that he held in his left hand, close to his left temple. He was leaning on something, perhaps the boat's wheel. "Now here," he said, pointing to the shot, "this is a gale of wind. Look at my eyeballs. I'm watching the gales. Watching the seas break." His expression was intent, free from distractions, oblivious to the cigarette's long ash.

I asked him if the reason he was watching them was that he had to keep the bow of the boat in a certain direction. I had been taught as a child to put the bow of my rowboat into the waves.

"Into the sea." He gestured forward with his right hand. "Instead of letting the boat get broadside to the sea, you don't get smashed up. You don't get the windows smashed out of the pilot house, the radar knocked off. You keep into the sea. It's a strain, but in the long run, you have no damage. The big seas will spread down both sides—won't come on deck. But if you got broadside and you get hit, you're going to have some damage, plus the stuff in the forecastle will be upset, the cook's stuff will be upset. Pots and pans, whatever he's got cooking—that will be on the other side of the boat."

I envisioned Mr. Patenaude, the cook, losing his footing, grabbing behind him at the refrigerator to brace himself, and watching with expletives a pot spill its contents on the forecastle floor.

"One of these seas hits you, I'm tellin' you, there's some power. There's no way can be figured out how much power is in those seas. If it hits you like this, down"—he forcefully lowered his hand toward the floor—"you're going to have damage. But if it happens to hit you with a push, like that"—he thrust his open hand out—"it will throw you away. But if the boat is heavy," he went on (I assumed that meant full of fish), "she's still going to take a hard crack. Something is going to give. Going into 'em—into the sea. It's a bad thing to run before a bad sea, because if it comes in over the stern, it's going to go the full length of the boat. If it breaks the doors in aft, then the boat is full of water."

I knew what that meant—a swamped engine room, a boat without power at the mercy of an angry sea, danger of sinking and possible loss of life. I pictured frantic fishermen and shuddered, grateful that there was no threatening storm to contend with on our imaginary trip aboard *Ellen Marie*.

Chapter 37
Fishing on
Ellen Marie

Captain Bowers fanned through the pages of *The Dragger* and stopped at a two-page photo of *Ellen Marie*'s starboard side leaning into a heavy sea. He drew my attention to a net piled in a heap on her slippery-looking deck near the rails. Atop the pile, several orbs that I imagined were bigger than softballs but smaller than soccer balls—floats, he said—would keep the top of the net's mouth raised above the sea bottom while *Ellen Marie* dragged for fish.

Beyond the net in the same picture, Captain Bowers pointed to dark shapes that he referred to as the *gallas* with the door in behind. I wasn't sure what he was pointing to and calling the gallas, but I saw a rectangular form that looked like a door. Its function was easy to grasp. *Ellen Marie* dragged the doors ahead of each side of the net to keep the mouth of the net wide open. The floats lifted the top of the net; pressure on the doors spread the mouth apart. I was glad that I had warned them that I knew nothing about commercial fishing because of my lack of visual or functional understanding of the gallas. But the captain must have assumed that I would recognize the terminology, for he moved quickly to another subject.

"This is where the wires come out," he said. "It holds the wires?" His upward inflection asked if I understood.

"Oh," I said in a descending groan that expressed waning hope of learning. I needed to learn the meaning of basic terms and functions that to him were commonplace, but, embarrassed, I had let myself be buried in a rush of the unfamiliar. Now I not only didn't understand gallas, but I also didn't understand what held the wires.

"Gallas," he repeated as if repetition would help. "There's one aft and one forward—the forward wire and after wire." As long as I had no understanding of the word, it didn't matter where they were.

Susan presented a different photograph, a full side view of *Ellen Marie*, which helped. "See these? Right there," she said, pointing to a tall, tubular metal structure shaped like an upside-down V. "That's the gallas."

Gallows on *Pocahontas* model in Maine Maritime Museum

The structure was clear. "Is it spelled *g-a-l-l-a-s?*" I finally asked. Captain Bowers corrected, *"G-a-l-l-o-w-s."*

"Gallows! Oh, okay," I said. They looked like you could hang something from them. I learned a new term, and I had the correct spelling. I sighed with relief.

"That's where the wire goes out," he continued. "One wire goes out through there, and the other wire comes here. Then, after you get them out, you throw a hook over."

I didn't know where either there or here was; nor could I conceptualize over what a hook was thrown. I kept quiet, thinking that it might be better to listen first and ask questions later, so the captain continued. "You pinch the two wires and put them inside of the hook, what you call the hookup block, and you put a pin in it. The two wires are in a small place where they stay in. Then they go out like this." He made a V shape with his arms. "Then you measure the depth of the water. Figure three to one."

"Three times depth for distance?" I asked.

"That's how much wire you put out," he said. "The wire is marked, most of them. First hundred fathom, mark ten then twenty. As it goes out, the guys keep track. Count the marks. Say you're fishing in fifty fathom. You have a hundred fifty outside the hookup block."

The math was simple, but it was obvious to Sue that I didn't understand the gear and how it worked to get the net out and hauled in. She said, "If you want to do this again, let us know." She seemed to realize better than I did that it would take more than one afternoon for me to grasp how everything worked on *Ellen Marie* from verbal and pictorial exposure to it.

Line Drawing of Net, Doors, and Eastern Rig from NEFSC, NOAA

For days after, I studied the interview that Captain Bowers had allowed me to record, with Bill Finn's pictures next to me for reference, and I located and read *White-Tipped Orange Masts,* the book that Dave Andrews had suggested. Sometimes I found answers to questions I hadn't thought to ask, such as what might be caught in the nets, also called otter trawls, besides fish—whale carcasses, old engines, anchors, huge rocks, shipwrecks, and human bodies. Gaining understanding was pure joy.

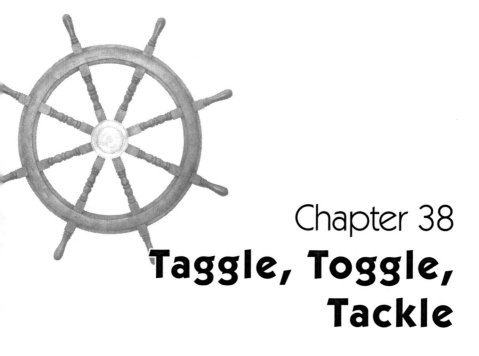

Chapter 38
Taggle, Toggle, Tackle

I wanted a NOAA chart of Nantucket Shoals and Georges Bank like the chart Susan had put in front of us when we took our imaginary trip. During my pursuit of one, a comedy of pronunciation variances—*taggle, toggle,* or *take-el*—unexpectedly led to greater understanding of how *Ellen Marie* hauled in her catch.

The source of NOAA charts I chose was C. E. Beckman's on Commercial Street in New Bedford within walking distance of the visitors center, Seaman's Bethel, Moniz Gallery, the Candleworks Restaurant, and the Whaling Museum—the area I had grown to love.

Seagulls squawked, and I smiled at their typical welcome to New Bedford. Jackhammering on Union Street, which ordinarily would have annoyed me, enhanced the high I felt from the warm summer day and the potential of acquiring a NOAA chart.

Parallel to Union, Commercial Street sloped toward the waterfront. I had walked a quarter of the way down when I noticed the C. E. Beckman sign at the far end of the street protruding from the gray stone building. A young man pulled a dolly stacked with boxes through a doorway, blocking the sidewalk while he loaded a truck. When I reached the dolly, I waited patiently. A second young man emerged from that doorway and asked politely what I was looking for. "C. E. Beckman's," I said. He wanted me to be more specific, so I told him that I wanted a NOAA chart. "That would be up this way," he responded. I hadn't realized that Beckman's business occupied the entire building along Commercial Street. I followed him along the sidewalk, retracing the steps I'd just taken past several doorways. I noticed their massive, hewn granite thresholds and wondered when they had been constructed.

The young man left me at a dusty counter in a dark, high-ceilinged room. I told the clerk what I wanted. Without a word, he turned in pursuit of the NOAA chart. Scanning the chamber, I noticed on one wall an abundance of little drawers, floor to ceiling, like the clear plastic ones that hold washers and screws in a modern hardware store. But these were not plastic; they were deep brown wood oiled by many fingers through years of use.

The clerk returned with the chart, which I purchased after verifying that it was similar to the one I had seen at Susan's. He rolled and secured it with an elastic band at each end, handed it to me, and disappeared once more before I had decided to ask a question. I sauntered toward the dark wood drawer wall and waited until I could speak with a different clerk, whom I overheard explaining to another customer that generations of Beckmans had operated the business. I envisioned whaling vessels in the harbor and customers at Beckman's dressed in tall collars and hats and the long, double-breasted coats of the 1850s.

When the clerk was available again, I asked, "Could you show me a taggle?" That was a term I had heard Captain Bowers use when he explained the process of hauling in *Ellen Marie*'s catch. His daughter Susan had repeated a different pronunciation that sounded like *take-el*. I hoped to gain understanding by seeing the object and perhaps hearing another explanation of its use.

"A taggle?" the clerk questioned. "I can show you a toggle, but I've never heard of a taggle. A taggle tale, maybe," he said in jest. "Tattle tale—taggle tale?" he repeated, raising his eyebrows as if I didn't get the joke. I wondered if Captain Bowers might have spelled it *t-o-g-g-l-e*.

The clerk held up a U-shaped piece of hardware with a pin through the legs of the U. "This is a toggle," he said as he held it out to me.

"How much is it?" I asked as I lifted and lowered it, surprised that its weight compared to two rolls of quarters. I considered displaying it on an end table or using it as a paperweight. He looked at me with furrowed brow as if he doubted my wisdom.

"It's going to cost a lot of money," he said. "That's bronze."

I gave it back regardless of its cost and left with my chart of Georges Bank. I was satisfied that although I didn't understand its use, I had seen a toggle.

Months before, at the Fishermen's Tribute Fundraiser, I had been introduced to Alan Cass. Alan had skippered *Ellen Marie* in the late '70s when owner Donald Calnan had her scalloping. A few days after my experience at C. E. Beckman's, Alan; his wife, Ann; and I rendezvoused at the Little Phoenix restaurant to talk about *Ellen Marie*. I asked Alan what the metal net was called that dragged for the scallops.

"The chain bag," he said, "made up of rings and links." He explained that in his day, fishermen would make up or repair the bag by holding the links with a pair of pliers or tweezers and slamming them shut with a hammer. The process changed around 1973 or 1974 to utilize implements called squeezers and cutters. I could tell that he was proud of the old-timers who could make them up faster with a hammer than a squeezer. He said, "If you told somebody to use a hammer and a pair of pliers today, they'd throw you over the side. But we turn around, we take one of the old *take-el* wires …"

"Spell *take-el*," I demanded, recognizing an opportunity to understand what Captain Bowers had referred to. Alan's momentary glare seemed to express annoyance at the interruption, but he responded to my request.

"*T-a-c-k-l-e*. Like tackle."

"That's not a toggle?" I asked.

"No. A toggle is different."

"Oh," I droned, disappointed that my research at C. E. Beckman's had been pointless.

Alan explained that a tackle (pronounced *take-el)* was a piece of line or wire that worked between two pulleys. Multiple pulleys were contained in a block. There was a deck block and a block above. The line going through the top block and coming down once was "one pull." Scallop draggers needed more strength than groundfish draggers. Multiple pulls provided the needed strength. The wire passed through the deck block and continued to the winch, the machinery that powered the hauling or letting go.

Alan asked for a pen. He drew a two-pull block on a paper napkin. We huddled above that napkin, Alan's wife, Ann, and I, as if our lives depended upon learning Alan's lesson. After the two-pull block, he illustrated the difference between tackle wire and tackle rope. He drew the winch and the gallows, which he phonetically spelled *g-a-l-l-i-s* on the napkin, and illustrated the configuration of the wires and drag relative to the boat.

It was making sense. I stopped being so hard on myself with unrealistic expectations and began comparing the learning process to pushing a car. It required tremendous effort to get a car rolling from a dead stop, but once it was rolling, the pushing got easier.

Winch on *Pocahontas* model at Maine Maritime Museum

Chapter 39
Final Puzzle Pieces

Alan Cass, like many others, went out of his way to help me learn. A few days after our Little Phoenix rendezvous, he took me to Leonard's Wharf in New Bedford, the last dock down to the south, where we boarded Wayne Frye's eastern-rig dragger, *Challenge*. We reviewed the path of the wires as they left the drums (winch) and went through the blocks (pulleys) over the bollards hanging from the gallows to the doors that would spread the mouth of the dragged net.

Alan explained, "Once the crew got the net all the way out, the captain would turn the boat so both wires come together, and on the stern there was a pelican hook. Both wires went through the pelican hook, you put the pelican on there, closed it, tied it off, and that way there she's towing off one spot off the stern. Then when he wanted to haul back, the guy goes back aft, takes the pin out of the pelican hook, hits it with a hammer, releases it—"

"Is there a pelican hook on here?" I interrupted.

"No, but I can show you one," he said and finished his thought. He explained that the pelican hook would split open and bring the wires apart and then the captain would turn the boat and haul back sideways.

"I don't know," he said, looking aft, "if there's a pelican hook around here somewhere." He turned around and looked down. "Here it is! That's a pelican hook."

The rusty hinged device, which had a ringed clasp secured by a pin, was right behind us on the deck. Alan picked it up and demonstrated the equipment. It was like a paralyzed hand, the fingers of which couldn't reach the thumb to enclose two cables. A ring, secured by its handle in the fingers, fit over the thumb, and a pin pierced the thumb to hold the ring in place. "Oh, Oh, Oh!" I said, expressing my delight of comprehension.

"Where would that be?"

"Aft. Off the king post aft, so that it could trap both wires."

"Captain Bowers talked about pinching the wires and putting them in a hook," I said. "That's it. I'll be darned." The puzzle was coming together.

Hallelujah! I understood!

Ellen Marie was an eastern-rig side trawler. *Eastern-rig* meant that her wheel house, or pilot house, was in the stern. Her net was dropped over the side, not from the stern. The lines ran from the power winch through the blocks to the gallows, to the doors, and beyond the doors to the net. When the net was dropped or hauled back, the line on one side of the net was guided through the bollard attached to the aft gallows, which was near the pilot house, and the line on the other side of the net was guided through the bollard attached to the forward gallows. *Ellen Marie* could fish from either port or starboard, something not all side trawlers could do. If her net was dropped and her lines went out on her port side (the left side), the Captain steered the boat starboard (right). That would bring the lines together, almost parallel and close to the boat. A crew member threw a hook over to grab both lines, which were drawn up and put into the pelican hook, secured to a post aft. From there the lines went out in the V shape that Captain Bowers had illustrated. In that way, *Ellen Marie* dragged the net from the stern, the doors kept the net wide, the floats kept the net open, and the fish went into the net. She brought her catch up by reversing the procedure.

I wouldn't say that my grasp of *Ellen Marie*'s gear and process was perfect, but I was happy with my understanding.

Chapter 40
Captain Ray Bono and the Fisherman's Feast

Aldo Eramo, my former co-worker, grew up in Boston's Italian North End and, as an adult, made his home there with his wife. He invited work friends to their parties, so I became acquainted with his family including his sister, Dina, who had married Raymond Bono, a Boston fisherman. It was this Raymond Bono, Raymie, who had said I could join one of his fishing trips until he wisely decided that insurance issues should prohibit it. So he left without me on that ill-fated trip that ended with a dramatic Coast Guard rescue and the loss of the *St. Jude*.

Captain Bono was intimately involved in the planning and orchestration of the annual North End Fisherman's Feast in honor of the Madonna del Soccorso. More than once, I experienced the four-day feast. I followed the statue of the Madonna for hours as she was carried along sausage- and souvenir-lined streets accompanied by the Roma Band. At dusk on Sunday, the final day of the feast, spectators anticipated the Flight of the Angel. The white-robed messenger, a girl perhaps twelve years old, flew in a harness from a second story window and hovered over the street, exclaiming, "Viva Maria!" The crowd looked up reverently as she delivered a discourse in Italian that ended with the release of white doves and a storm of confetti.

Many years had passed without contact with the Bonos, but it occurred to me one April day that Raymie might enjoy hearing about my *Ellen Marie* adventure, so, feeling both shy and excited, I called. Dina answered, jubilant over the reconnection. While I waited, she encapsulated my identity and purpose to Raymie before he took the phone. "Hi! It's so good to talk with you," I said in response to his hello.

"Good to hear from you. How've you been?" he asked.

I dove into my story about purchasing *The Pilot House* and how that led to a visit to South Bristol, Maine. Hearing of my experience at the Harvey Gamage Shipyard triggered his own memory of being there in 1958, three years before *Ellen Marie* was launched. He said he'd driven his father, Captain Vincenzo (Jimmy) Bono, and his father's partner to South Bristol to pick up their ninety-two-foot eastern rig, *Carmen & Vince,* a boat twelve feet longer than *Ellen Marie.* From a typically large and close-knit Italian family himself, Raymie said he'd been impressed by how many of the shipyard workers were Harvey Gamage's relatives.

We chatted about the fishing industry, the foreign trawlers, regulations, and Ray's experience as fishing-vessel captain. "The sea makes you humble," he said. I remembered Captain Bowers shaking his head left and right and saying, "There's no telling the power of the sea." I thought of the courage fishermen must have. We reminisced about good times in the North End as well. "Fifty-two years," Raymie said nostalgically. "I've been involved with the feast for fifty-two years."

Four months later, in August, I yearned to experience the annual Fisherman's Feast once more. On a hot Thursday evening, the first day of the feast, I found Ray's wife, Dina, in the middle of the crowded street waiting for the statue of the Madonna to be carried out of her chapel. Dina shouted over the clarinets, trumpets, and drums playing near us. "You know what's neat about this feast?" she said. "Everyone's related one way or another. Their parents or grandparents came from Sciacca, and they were all fishermen." I had read that fishermen from Sciacca, Sicily, had immigrated to America in the early 1900s and brought with them their devotion to the Madonna.

Sandwiched in the crowd waiting for the Madonna, I identified an eastern-rig dragger emblazoned on the back of the yellow t-shirt worn by a young man in front of me. I wouldn't have recognized it if I hadn't been researching *Ellen Marie*. A white banner with blue lettering, "In Memory of Deceased Fishermen," hung to the left of the chapel entrance. I stared at it with thoughts of Shelly in the New Bedford Harbor Commission office who had lost her Dad, of Anna who had lost her son, of the families who still mourned those who died when the *Lady of Grace* went down.

"Here she comes!" a child said. People stopped conversing and turned to watch the statue of the Madonna emerge from her sanctuary into a sea of clapping and cheering onlookers while the Roma Band continued to play. Two young men backed through the doorway toward the crowd, grasping in front of them the pole-sided platform bearing the statue of the Madonna. They and four others carefully maneuvered three steps while keeping her heavy-looking dais from tipping. The platform bearer closest to me, when he had firm footing on the street, gazed adoringly at the Madonna del Soccorso. White flowers and candles surrounded the blue-robed statue under a four-columned shelter, white trimmed with gold and covered with a gold crown flanked by two pink cherubs.

Madonna del Soccorso

Dina turned to me and said that Raymie credited the Madonna for saving his life twice; two of his boats had gone down. I winced and shook my head, wondering how they had endured such horrors. She handed me a long-stemmed red carnation and said, "Come on, Rae." Dina knew exactly where we should be as the procession marched to Christopher Columbus Waterfront Park for the blessing of the fishing waters.

Dina hesitated in the park and pointed to a granite stanchion. I looked at the post and saw "Capt. Ray Bono" in black lettering. "Oh! How nice," I said, wondering silently who had orchestrated the tribute and how. We continued to the waterfront, where we stood next to the stage. A priest prayed, "Have mercy on all families who have lost fishermen." I dropped the carnation into the fishing waters with all the others and added my heartfelt amen.

Chapter 41
The Siglers

Ray Bono had observed accurately that the Harvey Gamage Shipyard had been full of Harvey's relatives. Harvey's father-in-law, brother, three nephews, and several sons-in-law worked there for years. One of them was Don Sigler, whom I'd learned about from Alden Trull, the man who sold me *The Dragger*. He didn't know his last name, but he knew that a boat carpenter at Boothbay Harbor Shipyard, formerly Samples, had married Harvey Gamage's daughter and that he had worked at Gamage's. Alden wondered if Don might have helped build *Ellen Marie*.

I found Don unexpectedly through Peter Kass, whom I had read about in the online *Fisherman's Voice* article the night I first researched the Harvey Gamage Shipyard. I looked for Mr. Kass because the article mentioned that he had worked at Gamage's. When I reached him by phone, he said that he was too young to have worked on *Ellen Marie*, but he gave me Mr. Sigler's address and telephone number and suggested that I contact him. Don did remember working on *Ellen Marie*.

On the anniversary of my first visit to South Bristol, I returned with the hope of hearing Don Sigler tell me about *Ellen Marie*'s construction. I telephoned but had to leave messages. I stuffed my cell phone and digital camera into my pockets and leisurely walked from where I was staying on Sunset Loop past Island Grocery and down the State Road toward

Osier's. I never did visit Osier's that day. I found the historical society building open and went in. Displayed on the top shelf of a glass case was a portrait of Harvey Gamage and a blue oval medallion centrally emblazoned with his name: "Builder of Yachts and Motor Boats, South Bristol, State of Maine." I had my camera focused on them when my cell phone rang. It was Don. He said he was available to talk and invited me to his house in Bristol. I quickly departed, explaining to Mrs. Wells, the woman who oversaw the historical society and knew of my quest, that Don Sigler was available to talk about *Ellen Marie*'s construction.

Don, his wife Eunice, and I sat around their large round wooden table in their kitchen. Eunice's Maine roots were unmistakable when, in her thick accent, she said, "Don didn't know how to build a boat when he went there." She pronounced the word *they-uh*, meaning her father, Harvey Gamage's, shipyard. "He's from Maryland. Down south of Palmuh. Dad did take quite a few young men in they-uh," she explained, "and they learned the trade they-uh."

Don confirmed that he had learned boatbuilding from his father-in-law. "He was a very brutal man, but he was a nice guy," Don said of Harvey. "He looked right at me and said, 'Look, you got one goddamn boss around here, and that is me. Don't do nothin' anybody else tells ya.' And he meant what he said. He was the boss, and if somebody needed help, you didn't go help 'em. He would *tell* you go help 'em."

Eunice said, "My poor dad had six daughters before he had a son." She put her head back and laughed heartily.

Don, a rugged man with white hair, joked, "There wasn't none of 'em any good."

I asked Eunice if she had ever worked on any of the boats. She hadn't, but she said that her oldest sister had been secretary in the office when her father was building boats for the navy. Eunice laughed again. "We brought the husbands in. My next sister, Gertrude—her husband went to work they-uh when he got out of the service. My sister Dot's husband went to work they-uh when they got married." She laughed again.

Don patiently explained *Ellen Marie*'s construction including the frames, which I suggested were like ribs. "Well, see, we call 'em frames on a big boat," he said. He asked Eunice to get a writing tablet so he could help me to understand better through illustration. In addition to the tablet, she brought an impressive Warren Paper advertising brochure that featured color photos of Harvey Gamage's boat-building. I recognized the photo Elaine Coupe and I had seen in Camden of the *Appledore* being built in the big gray shed. Someone had written "Eunice Sigler" on the front upper right corner of the brochure. Don took the opportunity to joke. "I don't know why they got her name on it. She didn't have a damn thing to do with them boats." I laughed. We were relaxing into friendship.

I read aloud a list I'd written of tools I had seen at the Maine Maritime Museum—tools used in schooner construction in the late 1800s. I asked if similar tools had been used in *Ellen Marie*'s construction. Don said yes to most of them. When I mentioned a lining adze, Don said, "That was one of my last jobs down there—line the boat." He explained the purpose of the lining adze—so the plank would lie flat. "We done the frames that way. Flattened little places off on the frames."

Don told me about bolts called *drifts*. I asked if they were steel. "Yes. Yes," he said. "The only boat we built down there that we used wooden trunnels on was the *Edgartown*. It was a big scalloper."

"Dad was famous for his dragg-uhs and scallop-uhs," Eunice said. "That's the reason the National Science Foundation had him build the *Hero*. She was a dragg-uh. See? But they built her like twice as heavy for Antarctica."

I took the bait. "Why did they want the dragger design for the *Hero?*" I asked.

"They dragged down they-uh. Research!" she said. "See, they worked in ice. That boat had to be able to give. That's one reason they wanted wood, not metal. She worked down they-uh during some cold spells. And they wanted a boat that would give."

Eunice's reference to metal boats led me to ask when the builders installed the metal, meaning the gallows and the winch, on *Ellen Marie*. Don explained that after the deck was caulked, a gallows pad went on, and then they bolted on the gallows, which came from Hathaway Winch in Fairhaven, Massachusetts.

"Hathaway Winch went out of business," he said. "There was some man killed on a boat, and they blamed it on the winch that Hathaway produced for the boat, and they sued 'em. It was a big company too. Got everything they had. Her Daddy bought hundreds of winches from 'em."

The distance between Bristol, Maine, and Fairhaven, Massachusetts, suddenly seemed to shrink.

I told Don and Eunice what I had heard from Captain Bowers—that Mr. Gamage had guessed that the captain was from Lunenberg, Nova Scotia, because the captain requested a break deck, which all Lunenberg schooners had.

Don began to explain. "Well, that was ... Let me see ..."

"I know what a break deck is," I interrupted. "A raised deck that directs the sea that comes over the bow out the scuppers." He seemed relieved not to have to explain that one. I told them about my visit to the Grand Banks Schooner Museum in Bath where I'd boarded the *Sherman Zwicker*. While below deck, I had realized from an address on a shipping crate that the *Sherman Zwicker* was a Lunenberg schooner, so I had hurried topside to find the break deck.

"A step was all it was," Don said, minimizing the construction challenge. I remembered feeling prideful when I found the break deck on the *Sherman Zwicker*, believing that not many other visitors would know its purpose.

I didn't intend for my next question to be shocking. "Does a boat always have to have water in the very bottom?" I asked, thinking of the *Regina Maris*, the barkentine I'd called home while conducting coral research in St. John. I remembered a crew member using a stick through a hatch in the forecastle floor to measure the depth of water in the hull.

"Wat-uh?" Eunice inquired incredulously. "Wat-uh get in, they pump it out. They don't want wat-uh!" As informed as I was about things like break decks, I was naïve about others. It was a good thing that I hadn't realized when I was on *Regina* that she'd had a leaking problem.

Their announcement that concrete was in *Ellen Marie*'s fish hold surprised me about as much. I thought there must be a limit to how much a boat could weigh and stay afloat. Don described how he and Eunice's brother-in-law would mix the cement, carry it onto the boat in five-gallon buckets, lower it with rope, and dump it. Harvey would give them a line on the boat, and they'd add the concrete until the spot that Harvey had marked became level with the water. "He'd watch the line on the copper paint," Don said. "He'd tell us, 'Well, you gotta have more aft.' He'd say, 'Drop the ass of her down,' or, 'Put the nose of it down.'

So if he wanted the bow down, we'd put more forward. If he wanted the stern down, we'd put more aft."

Somewhere I had gotten the idea that there was a blacksmith shop at the shipyard, so I asked if that was true. "Oh, yuh," Don confirmed. "Blacksmith shop, machine shop ..." They were needed for fuel tanks, mast stems, piping, and water tanks. Part of Don's job was to take the water tanks to Bath Iron Works to have them galvanized.

"Who did the finish carpentry work on *Ellen Marie?*" I asked.

Both Eunice and Don thought that it was Eunice's grandfather, Myles Plummer. "Mumma's father," she said. "He done 90 percent of the finish carpentry work for quite a long time down they-uh. Dad had a lot of his relatives working." That made her laugh again.

"Somebody down in New Bedford told me that your father used to put silver dollars under the mast," I said. "Was that true?"

"Uh-hum," answered Eunice.

"Yup," Don confirmed, "He always done that himself. He wouldn't give it to his brother or nobody. He'd be right there. Because he said, 'I know you sons of bitches would steal it.' But he's right there, and just before they set it down, he'd drop it in there and then they'd set the mast down. He said, 'Now I know you can't get it.'" I wondered if it was a 1961 silver dollar that Harvey had locked between *Ellen Marie*'s deck and mast.

I asked Don if he had made *Ellen Marie*'s dories.

"Yuh, I used to. Her daddy got me in all kind of goddamn messes, 'cause he knew I'd work. But I used to saw everything out for the dories down to the shop evenings or Saturdays or Sundays—saw out the frames, the stern, the plank, the bottom, all that—and I'd load 'em in my truck and then take 'em over here on River Road to a man named Merritt Francis, and he would put 'em together."

I had one last question. "Why were the dories and the masts orange?"

"For color," Don explained. "So that the Coast Guard could see you way off."

"Ohhh." My voice rose and fell like a siren. I told Don and Eunice that the orange color was why I originally had been drawn to *The Pilot House*.

"Binoxi orange was the name of it," Don remembered. "You could get that damn stuff on your hands, but you could *not* get it off."

I didn't want to leave without Don's tablet page of illustrations of the frames, water tanks, bilge stringer, and clamps, so I asked, "May I rip this out?"

"Sure," he said, adding, poker-faced, "That ain't very good drawin'. Don't tell anybody I drew it."

I promised to put his name right on it.

Chapter 42
Edward T. Gamage, Boatbuilder, and *Ellen Marie's* Launching

The timing of meeting *Ellen Marie's* builders was like going from stern to stem instead of stem to stern, but that's the way this adventure unfolded. Edward T. Gamage, Eunice Sigler's cousin, and his wife, Bunny, welcomed me to their Damariscotta home the same week I met the Siglers. Edward had worked for twenty-nine years at Gamage before he began his own shipyard. When I told Edward that I had met Don Sigler, he said, "Don was the smartest guy they had over at Samples for a while. They hated to see him leave too, I'll tell ya."

Edward described two Gamage Shipyard crews of at least six men each: the wood crew, directed by Harvey himself, and the "black gang," called that because they did the blacksmithing—installing engines, piping, and wiring. Edward had taken over the black gang after his father died.

Of Harvey, Edward said, "He pushed that old planer. Boy, you could hear it hummin' all over the island. The planer was set up to take a quarter of an inch. Harvey had to take three-eighths. He would have four, five men pushing it to get it through there. Instead of putting it through once and bringin' it back. He didn't want to bring it back and put it through again." (Because it would have cost time, I guessed, and time was money.) "Harvey done a hell of a lot of work. What he done, it would take three men to keep up with him. I'll tell ya."

Ellen Marie had been in the hands of some hardworking men.

Bunny, who sat to my left at their kitchen table, urged her husband to tell me what he had done to Alden Manchester. I looked to my right at Edward.

"Oh," he said. "This friend of ours down at McFarland's Cove, Alden Manchester and his wife—they wanted to go to Boothbay. I had a small lobster boat—twenty-eight-foot lobster boat. I says, 'All right. I'll take you over.' We went over. It was early in the evening. We got ready to come home. Of course, it was pitch dark, so we come up through … You've heard of the Thread of Life?"

I hadn't, so he told me about the mile-long channel formed by a string of islands to the east of the Rutherford Island section of South Bristol.

"We come from Boothbay across. We come up through the Thread of Life, and Alden said, 'How do you know where you're goin'? You can't see nothing.' I said, 'Oh, we're all right. You wait a few minutes, there's a buoy. I'll go right up to that buoy so you can see it. We got up there, and I said, 'There's the buoy.' I says, 'You wait a few minutes, there will be one over there.' So we went a few minutes. I said, 'You watch. That one will come up over there.' Shook his head. He said, 'Now how the hell you know where them buoys are? You can't see 'em.' I said, 'Alden, the gulls land on there all the time. All you got to do is sniff, and you can go right for the smell.'"

"And he believed it," Bunny said, chuckling.

"He believed every word of that," Edward agreed. "I never told him the difference. 'All you got to do is just go like that, and you'll smell them buoys right out, Alden.'" I looked at my recorder in the center of the table, grateful that I had asked permission to turn it on.

At my request, Edward patiently educated me about *Ellen Marie*'s launching, which he pronounced *lanchin'*. What I called rails he named the sliding way and the launching way. An oak holding strip attached to both ways kept the sliding way from moving. I grabbed a brown envelope from my briefcase, from which I removed *Ellen Marie*'s launching photos and handed them to Edward. He pointed to the cradles on each side of her keel, explaining that at launching time, the crew drove rough-sawed oak wedges into the cradle structures that lifted the boat. When they sawed through the oak holding strip that had immobilized the sliding way, she began to move through the doors of the big gray shed into the icy North Atlantic waters. Edward shuffled the pictures until the photo of *Ellen Marie* sliding into the harbor was on top.

"That's Edward right there," he said, referring to himself in the third person, pointing to the man with the line in his hands on *Ellen Marie*'s bow.

"You? That's you?" I asked. "I'll be darned." That connection worked like magic. I felt like I had been teleported into that February day in 1961 with one foot still in the present.

"See that line right there?" Edward asked, drawing attention to the rope he held in his hands in the picture. "In South Bristol, you know the distance from the shed doors to the back over there?"

I nodded, picturing the distance across the harbor. "This boat was doin' about fifteen miles an hour when she hit the water, so we had this snub line that come up here where I was, and the minute it got out so far, I had to take the turns on the bit to slow it down."

"On the bit," I repeated.

"Yuh. So it wouldn't go across the harbor."

"What's the bit?" I asked.

"Well, that's a big steel pipe thing that stands up on the deck to tie the boat up to? And, uh, I had to put four, five turns on there. And the smoke would roll right off it. It would burn the rope. We couldn't use the rope over again, 'cause it was burnt. That's how you had to stop 'em, or they would go on the ledges over across the cove there. You look, you'll see the shed over to the other shore. There ain't much room."

"What was it tied to on this end?" I asked.

"The pilin' under the dock. Down at the low water mark. So he'd get the strength right there. Them pilings, some of them are drove in the mud there twenty feet. So you get right down low water, put the rope over, and tie it right next to the mud. That's where all the strength was. That's what stopped it."

Joseph Perry, who had purchased *Ellen Marie* for Captain Woodie Bowers, had traveled to Maine for the launching. According to Edward, "It was a hell of a snowstorm. Mr. Perry stayed over at the Newcastle Inn, and he got so far as the golf course and he got stuck in a snowbank. Well, it come time for the lanchin', and Harvey lanched the boat. So he got down there about an hour after the boat was in the water. He come down through that yard … I can see him comin' now, in through that shop, and Harvey was standing there. He says, 'Mr. Gamage,' he says, 'this is not like buying a can of beans. Why did you lanch that boat?' And Harvey looked at him and said, 'Well, I tell ya,' he says, 'time and tide waits for no man.' That was that. The argument was over right there."

Edward announced that he was going out to his shed to get something. A few minutes later, he returned with a roughhewn oak wedge like those that had lifted *Ellen Marie*. "Here," he said. "You can say that this lanched the boat."

"For me?" I asked, putting my hand to my chest.

He nodded. "If you want it. Some people sand 'em down and hang 'em on a wall."

"Sure. I want it. Thank you!" I reached for the aged wood wedge that would have been a four-by-four-inch square post three feet long had the sides not gradually tapered down its length to nothingness. But Edward suggested that he lay it on the kitchen floor for now. I acquiesced.

Before I packed my belongings, I showed Bunny and Edward a picture I had taken of a small island in the mist next to Coveside Inn in South Bristol. I thought it was one of my better photographs. Edward said, "I tell you what they've done. They've moved that in there since I was a boy. That wasn't there. They moved that in there."

"What?" I questioned.

"That island," he said without cracking a smile.

"Oh, Edward!" Bunny said.

"That wasn't ever there," he persisted. "They must have moved it in."

If I hadn't heard the Alden Manchester story, I might have fallen victim to Edward's humor, but I didn't. I sensed the smile in his heart. That, and the gratitude in my own, fertilized two more special friendships.

Chapter 43
More Coincidences

Throughout my research, the strangest things happened whenever I mentioned *Ellen Marie* in casual conversation. For example, one day Rob Gomes, a fellow regular at The Little Phoenix Restaurant, took the vacant counter stool next to me. When I referred to my *Ellen Marie* research, he said, "You have to talk to my father-in-law." He wrote the name Jim Holden and a phone number on a slip of paper and slid it toward me. Shortly after he departed, the restaurant phone rang. Sarah, the owner, answered, walked toward me with the phone in her outstretched hand, and said, "It's for you." It was Rob. He'd spoken with his in-laws, and they were looking forward to my call.

That night, when I telephoned Mr. Holden, I learned that he had been a principal in Hathaway Ice, which had loaded *Ellen Marie* with about ten tons of ice before each trip to preserve the fish she would catch. Jim shared many stories about the New Bedford waterfront. After Don Sigler told me that Hathaway Winch was the source of *Ellen Marie's* winch and gallows, I called Jim a second time to ask if he knew about the company. He confirmed Don's story of the failed business but corrected the name to Hathaway Machine.

Another coincidence occurred one Sunday while I was eating lunch alone at a restaurant in Walpole, Massachusetts. The manager, Jay

Levenson, inquired about my meal satisfaction. He lingered to chat briefly. When I mentioned that my work and hobby often vied for my time, he asked what my hobby was. Of course, I told him about *Ellen Marie*. "My uncle owned Ell Vee Dee in New Bedford," he said. "I worked there when I was a kid."

"You're joking," I responded. "*Ellen Marie* sold her fish to Ell Vee Dee."

He explained that his dad had been a Dartmouth attorney whose clients included boat owners, some of whom had invited his mother to christen their boats. At another time, I showed him the picture of the woman who christened *Ellen Marie* to see if it was his mother, but it wasn't.

I was beginning to surrender to the likelihood that *Ellen Marie*'s christener would remain a mystery. But like a candle flame that refuses to be extinguished, the topic unexpectedly arose when I was in South Bristol visiting David and Betsy Andrews. I don't know who was more surprised—David that I believed there were no regular launching articles or I that he had a collection of them. When we discovered that his collection included launchings only up to 1958, David, a motivated detective himself, called the *Lincoln County News* office to verify availability of newspapers from 1961.

When we arrived at the office, the huge bound volume of newspapers was set out on a counter. Hope faded quickly as I turned page after page without seeing one photo of an eastern-rig dragger. David began flipping pages backward. He stopped at the front page of the February 9 edition, and suddenly, when I saw the words he pointed to, I felt a surge of elation: "*Ellen Marie* Slides Down Ways …"

"The person who christened the vessel was called a sponsor," David said.

There it was—the information I had thought lost forever. "The dragger, sponsored by Mrs. Charles Radcliffe of Fairhaven, Mass. …" Within days, thanks to a chain of helpful Fairhaven individuals, I was able to reach Lillian (Radcliffe) Langill in Florida by telephone. She explained how she happened to sponsor *Ellen Marie*.

"My husband worked at the bank in Fairhaven," she said. "Joseph Perry did business with him. Mr. Perry asked me if I would like to christen the boat."

Chapter 44
Her Last Owner

There was another person I hadn't found—*Ellen Marie*'s final owner. My past attempt to find him had been thwarted by technological difficulties. I called the Rhode Island secretary of state's office again, hoping that this time their computers were operational so I could get the information I wanted. The clerk told me that Little Fishery Inc. had been dissolved in 1991. "That's all we have," she said.

Frustrated, I pressed for more. "You don't have any listing of the principals of the corporation?"

She hesitated and then added, "Branimir Viducic was the president."

"Yes! That's what I was looking for. Thank you."

The Internet was generous with its information about Mr. Viducic. He answered the telephone himself when I called his home in Old Orchard Beach, Maine—yet another coincidence in my search for *Ellen Marie*, for Mr. Viducic said that he was rarely at home but was there recuperating from neck surgery.

I told him that I had heard that the boat sunk. "Is it true?"

"Yes. I was not the skipper then," he said with an accent that hinted of his Croatian roots. "My brother-in-law was the skipper. There was an oil stove on her for heat. It caught on fire. She sank off Block Island in 1989."

He changed the subject. "Have you read the book *Dead Men Tapping*? I'm in the book."

When I admitted that I hadn't, he told me briefly about the horrific tragedy at sea involving fishing vessel *Heather Lynne II*.

He had changed the boat's name from *Ellen Marie* to *Three Vs*. I asked him the significance of the new name.

"I renamed the boat after my three children," he said. "We fished out of either Newport or New Bedford. When I first bought the boat, I moved the boat from Fairhaven. I had it tied up at the Hathaway Ice side. I was welding at the pier. I had already put the name *Three Vs* on it. A man stopped and asked, 'What was the name of this before?' I told him some crazy name. He said, 'Nah … you can't kid me. I know.' The man was Woodie Bowers."

I remembered Captain Bowers's daughter's comment that it was bad luck to change the name of a boat.

"The boat was switched over," he continued. "It wasn't designed for scalloping. She had a bigger engine put in her. After that, she sat down in the stern more." I remembered Don Sigler talking about Harvey Gamage marking *Ellen Marie* and directing the crew to add cement until she sat just so. "I used to own a steel boat in 1980," Bronko said. "When the lease expired, I bought that boat."

I told him about my trip to South Bristol when I had spoken with a fisherman who had given me the National Marine Fisheries phone number.

"David Osier?"

"Yes," I responded incredulously. "How did you know?"

"He's a good friend. I just talked to him."

Amazed, I asked, "Do fishermen know all fishermen?"

"Fishermen," he said, "we hang around together."

Again, he talked about the boat. "I took a hatch off her and made a table. I changed the forecastle. It had a triangle table. I took that out. I took the side beds out. I saved the table. It was polished oak."

I told him about going to see *Rianda*.

"The *Rianda* was *way* bigger than *Ellen Marie*. She was more like the *Susan B* or the *Columbia*. The *Columbia* was the last wood boat built in 1980."

Columbia at pier 3 in New Bedford in 2007

That phone conversation milled around in my head until I finally admitted that I still wasn't sure of *Ellen Marie*'s fate because of his comments about changes in the forecastle and about taking a hatch off her. I wondered if she had been raised, towed in, and repaired.

Chapter 45
Finding Captain Heflin

It was a quiet Sunday afternoon. I was lounging in my *Pilot House*–inspired terra cotta–colored swivel chair with my feet up on the ottoman, reading *Dead Men Tapping*. I was so surprised to find not just a name drop but a whole chapter about Bronko Viducic's role in the loss of the *Heather Lynne* that I called to tell him so.

By the end of the conversation, I had three ways to find, possibly, someone who had experienced what might have been the boat's last day afloat. The most logical one to start with was the name of the *Three Vs* skipper, James Heflin, with whom Mr. Viducic had lost contact. If that didn't work, I could go to Salas's, a waterfront bar that once had been a hangout for the crew in Newport, Rhode Island, the boat's last port city. The third clue was a long shot—I could try to contact someone from a fishing boat from Point Judith that had been on scene when *Ellen Marie/Three Vs* was in trouble.

The Internet yielded nine pages of James Heflins across America but none in Rhode Island or Massachusetts. I called Alabama, Maine, New Jersey, Maryland, and seven cities in Texas without success before I set the list aside to try a different approach.

I called Salas's. The man who answered gave me the direct number that rang in the bar. I told the bartender about my quest and asked if she would be willing to hang a poster if I brought her one.

"Sure. I could do that," she said.

Using red in Microsoft Publisher, I typed, "Mayday!" Then, switching to black, I wrote, "Did you fish on the scalloper Three Vs when she sank in 1989? Do you know someone who did? Please call ..."

I also made one last effort to get information from the Coast Guard by filing a Freedom of Information Act Request on August 10. Over the months of my search, I had contacted almost as many Coast Guard offices as I had numbers for James Heflin, with similar results. Incident reports that went back farther than the Coast Guard's entrance into the magic age of computers, if the reports existed at all, seemed impossible to locate. There were no Coast Guard personnel who might remember the 1989 episode in Point Judith, Newport, or other key locations because of frequent rotation as well as the passage of time.

I had gleaned the specific date of the incident, March 22, 1989; the Coast Guard case number; and the e-mail address to which to send the FOIA request. I asked for any and all documentation, especially names of crew members and the identity of the boat to which the crew was transferred. With a sigh of accomplishment and hope, I filed my printed copy in the Coast Guard folder and returned it to my cardboard box of *Ellen Marie* research files between Cass and Corporations/Ownership.

I called my friend Dwight. "I'm going over to Newport to a fishermen's bar. You want to go?" I expected that he would, and I knew I would be more comfortable if I wasn't alone. Newport was teeming with tourists, but the area behind the bar was quiet. I pulled the car into a convenient parking space next to the rear entrance of the bar. The door was propped open—a black door painted with a white skull wearing a red bandana, white crossbones, and the multicolored name Tropical Bar. The bartender blended into the pirate décor with her black hair, tattoos, and nose ring. She took my poster and left in its place the soda water I ordered. Strangely, I felt at home. There were only three men in the place in addition to Dwight, two on stools at the bar, one standing. After I told the man sitting next to me why I was there, he suggested that I ask Louis Parascandolo at the end of the pier about the *Three Vs*. I said that I would. The soda water was on the house.

Salas's on Newport's popular Thames Street

Dwight and I walked toward the end of the pier, passing several Parascandolo box trucks, and climbed a steep stairway that led to the office. We entered, and I explained why we were there.

Louis and Nickie Parascandolo, two of five brothers, continued to operate their father's fish transportation business, though they looked like they were old enough to retire. Mike, the third generation, remembered a visit two months prior from James Heflin. "Little James" they called him. Nickie, a hefty, white-haired man, searched the Newport phone directory with no better results than my own while Mike called someone in the plant to see if he could come up with James's location or place of employment. The most they remembered was that he worked for some glass company, possibly in the New Bedford area.

Nickie seemed to enjoy talking about the old times. He remembered *Ellen Marie*, "a beautiful, beautiful vessel" in his opinion, and her captain, Woodie Bowers. "Quite a fisherman," he said. "He made a pile of money with that boat." He recalled that Woodie used to sell to Ell Vee Dee and that Nickie himself delivered some of the fish to New York. His reminiscing drew a picture of change. The Newport docks were no longer heaped with coal, the fishermen were not quite as tough as they used to be, and the supply of fish "not a sixteenth" of what used to be around. They wished me well in my search for Little James.

I felt like a detective on television's *Law and Order* when I was calling New Bedford–area glass companies to ask for James Heflin. I liked the role, but it didn't lead to the man. I went back to searching names on the Internet, where I widened my search for any Heflin and narrowed the search to Rhode Island. I called a number for a female Heflin in Newport. A male answered. At first, I thought I had found the skipper, but he said, "I've never been on a boat." Only then did I realize that I was talking with a youngster. After a moment of hesitation, he said, "It could be my father." He suggested an evening time to call back. By then, his mother had been authorized to give me his father's cell phone number. That's how I found Little James Heflin, the skipper who lived through the tragedy of *Ellen Marie*, the *Three Vs*.

Chapter 46
Day of Tragedy

The ringing of my cell phone was almost obscured by the din in Newport's Tropical Pirate Bar. Little James Heflin was calling to tell me that he was approaching the rear entrance. I left my table near the front windows, ambled past the bar and the wall-mounted deer head with its tricorner hat and eye patch, and made my way to the open rear door, where I saw a slim young-looking man with a cell phone up to his ear walking toward the steps.

"Hi. I guess you're James," I said, wondering if he felt as silly as I did talking in person yet still holding a cell phone to an ear. It was too noisy in the bar to record a conversation. Since it was a beautiful sunny day, we walked toward Parascandolo's on the dock. On the way, I learned that *Three Vs* had tied up at this same quay. James asked to be reminded of the boat's name before she was *Three Vs*. To me, her name was and would always be *Ellen Marie*. I couldn't bring myself to call her anything else. I didn't like that Bronko had renamed her and would like to have reminded him that it was bad luck to change the name of a boat. Ninety-nine percent of me didn't believe it, but 1 percent wondered about a connection between the name change and the boat's demise.

James offered me a seat on the back of his red pickup truck, which was parked in the middle of the pier. The tailgate creaked as he opened it. Gulls were squawking, and a soft breeze wafted as we settled into an easy flow of conversation. In his Louisiana accent, James explained that he had returned to the area to be with his kids. "You talked with James Junior on the phone," he said.

"Yuh," I responded. "At first I thought I was talking to you, until he said, 'I've never been on a boat.'" We laughed.

"So you want to know why I've been chasing this down?" I asked. I followed his enthusiastic response with my story of *The Pilot House*, my passion that bloomed to find her, and my search that began in South Bristol.

"Really!" he said. "Where you at?"

"I'm at the day she sank." We laughed again.

"The day she sank, we left out of here."

"What kind of a day was it?"

His description of cold weather and real rough seas contrasted with the comfort we were experiencing on that blue-sky September afternoon. He paused, naming crew members as if he had to think about who had been on the boat. "We had just come in … Did Bronko tell you anything about it?"

"Very little," I said.

"Let me back up a little bit. We had just come in, because there was a real bad northeaster blowin', and we laid up off of Fire Island for five days."

"Wow. That's a long storm," I said, picturing the boat south of Long Island near Fire Island beach.

"It was bad!" he said. "Everybody was icing up. Boats were going down. It was really bad. Really bad. Anyway, the storm—we laid up on the beach. I told the engineer to go down and start the engine. It had an old air starter in it. We had air tanks and an air starter. As soon as the generator kicked in to recharge that thing, all the fire went out. I mean we lost all our power. We set there for another three days. The storm was just raging. We finally talked the Coast Guard into coming out. They didn't want to. It was so bad. They were busy rescuing boats and stuff. Anyway, they came to get us. I had one of my dredges from my main wire right up on the beach. Set the dredge and then drifted offshore, so I had all my wire run out. Bronko had just put brand-new dredge, brand-new cable. The Coast Guard said, 'Look. We're here to pull you in. You either cut that wire, or we're leaving.' And I had no power. That boat was a chunk of ice. I mean that boat was just a *huge* chunk of ice. I wound up cuttin' the cable. They pulled us in … I want to say to Point Judith. I may be wrong. Bronko worked on the boat and brought it back over here. He wired up a new generator right here. Couple days later," he continued, "we left."

So just days prior to her fateful day of March 22, 1989, *Ellen Marie,* then known as *Three Vs,* and her crew had experienced a dreadful north-easter, loss of power and gear, and a Coast Guard tow to port. I asked James where he had been headed when they left Newport again.

"We were going to work off New York. We had to go back off Fire Island where we anchored up and catch our dredge. I left our dredge and all our brand-new cable sitting on the bottom of the ocean. I had to go back and catch it."

James clicked open a silver lighter and lit a cigarette. I thought of the submerged chain bag, as Alan Cass had called it, and how upset Bronko must have been when he learned that James had had to cut it loose. A screeching seagull swooped down and landed at the edge of the dock.

"It was late at night," he continued. "We weren't far off Point Judith. I could see the light," he said, referring to the lighthouse located at the west side of the entrance to Narragansett Bay. "And when we turned the point, we could see the Coast Guard's light. Later, I was in the bunk asleep. Dennis came in. 'There's a fire in the engine room.' I opened up the door. My bunk room had a door went right straight down to the engine room. When I opened it up, flames came up. When it caught that wind, the air, it just blew up there and singed all the hair off my face and stuff."

"How was the fire discovered?"

"Dennis was in the wheelhouse and saw smoke. Well, on the old eastern rigs—well most of 'em—there was a vent, right? On those old eastern rigs, it comes out right in front of the wheelhouse. He saw smoke coming out."

"There wasn't anybody in the engine room at the time?"

"No. That's where he slept. And I slept right above it, right behind the wheelhouse. But everybody else slept … all the crew's quarters were up forward."

"In the fo'c'sle," I said, purposely exaggerating the pronunciation.

"Yuh," James said, repeating the same inflection. We smiled at each other.

"He come runnin' in, saying, 'There's smoke.' I guess he didn't realize the fire was going on until—I mean, the second I jumped out of my bunk, I went to go down the engine room. The flames were all the way up to the top."

"So bad that you got burned."

"Yup. The crew didn't have a clue what was going on at that time, 'cause they were up forward. I told him to go get everybody up. I start chunking survival suits at 'em. They were all upstairs. We had one more man than there were survival suits. I threw all the survival suits out."

"What did you think when you realized that you had one too few survival suits?"

"I knew I was going to get cold." His strong laugh burst forth again. "I was in the wheelhouse talking to the Coast Guard, telling them where we were at and what was going on."

"What were you thinking?"

"I was afraid everybody was going to have to get in the water, and ... I don't know. It happened so fast. I wasn't scared, but I was worried. The fire was in the back of the boat, and we had a bunch of oxygen and acetylene tanks back there. I just knew it was fixing to explode. We couldn't get to the raft sittin' on the back of the boat, which was on fire. And, uh, all I had on was a pair of long john pants. No socks. No shoes. No shirt. No nothin'." He laughed a hearty laugh. "But I looked up, and I saw the blue light—the Coast Guard—so I went out on deck with the guys."

James said that a boat with an anchor sticking out of the bow, typical of southern boats, had responded to his Mayday. I remembered Bronko saying that there had been a fishing boat from Point Judith there.

"He was tryin' to get to us to pull us off the boat, and the seas were real big, and his anchor dug into the bow of the *Three Vs*. When the seas came up, it just ripped a big chunk off the front of the boat. Ha ha ha. 'Get back, man!' I don't remember who they were," he said. "I've never talked to them since."

I thought of my *Ellen Marie* struggling at sea with her bow torn up, and I felt sad.

"It was just a few more minutes when the Coast Guard got to us. We didn't have to get in the water."

I had to ask James which boat rescued the crew—the fishing vessel or the Coast Guard boat. They had transferred to a small Coast Guard boat.

"We stayed, put the fire out. They just flooded the boat. The fire was on the stern, and they had pumps on the Coast Guard boat, and they just kept pumping the water in there. You could tell the boat was taking on a bunch of water. The whole back end was burnt out. When we left, it was just adrift. They wanted us to get a towboat and go back out to get it. They took us in to Point Judith. My sister picked us up, brought us back over here."

I wondered how much time had elapsed between the fire's discovery and the rescue.

"They was there real fast," James said. "We weren't that far off Montauk, 'cause we were making the curve. I was staying close to the beach, because I was going back up on the beach off Fire Island to get the dredge. Normally we pull out of Newport, we go straight east, but ..."

"East?" I interrupted.

James explained that back in those days they usually fished out at Georges Banks—the channel—wherever they wanted to go.

When I asked him what it was like getting off *Three Vs* onto the Coast Guard vessel, I expected a description of the physical transfer, but he expressed not liking it for two reasons. Not only was it the boat they worked on, but it was his family's boat.

"When you went off onto the Coast Guard boat, was it just like going from one boat to the other when they're tied up next to each other?"

"Yes. They pulled right up to us. I mean, it was rough."

James stopped to answer his cell phone. Its ring tone was "Mexican Hat Dance," which was comical in light of his next revelation about a crew member who was a Mexican immigrant.

"He was illegal," he said, "but he had been shrimpin' all his life. But he was on the boat. His name was Oscar. But old Oscar ... You know there's a big tire they tie the boats up with? Not the inner tube—the tire. We had one on the bow. I look up. I'm talking to the Coast Guard on the radio, and there's Oscar standing on the bow of the *Three Vs*. The thing had to be more than a hundred pounds. He had that tire around him.

'No, Oscar! You jump off with that, you're going to go straight down.'"
James laughed again.

"Where was the Coast Guard coming from?"

"Point Judith. They were there real quick. I didn't have time to do anything. I was talking to them. They kept asking questions, you know. The smoke was so ... that old wood was soaked with oil and diesel for so many years, the smoke was noxious. I was hanging out the window trying to talk to them. It was billowing out past my head. I couldn't breathe. But it happened real fast. It really did."

Thinking back to the first time I saw *The Dragger*, and how alive *Ellen Marie* looked with the smiling crew member leaning out the starboard wheelhouse window, I wanted to know from which window the suffering James had been leaning. The question seemed petty, even disrespectful, but I asked anyway. "Do you remember which window you were hanging out?" The effect of the question was dramatic.

"Yuh. I was ... I was ..." James hesitated for a long time. I chose to be silent to see what would happen. I was glad I did, because James changed. It was as if he was actually reliving the drama. "Yuh," he said and then laughed a different, quiet, subdued laugh. "I remember every bit of it. I remember talking on the radio. All the guys were right down here below putting on survival suits, and, uh, Oscar was up on the bow with that damn tire." He laughed again reservedly.

"What color were those survival suits?" I asked him.

"Orange. They were all orange. I guess so they can be easily seen. I wound up ... The Coast Guard gave me one of their wetsuits. One of those real fancy wet suits? I didn't have any clothes, so I ended up wearing it home. I had that thing for another fifteen years before I got rid of it." Suddenly, he straightened his posture. "No, it was Block Island! It had Block Island Coast Guard on it. Block Island was the Coast Guard."

A Harley Davidson had been idling near Parascandolo's. When it revved, I turned and watched it leave the pier while James explained that he had asked someone named Freddie if he would be willing to pull in the swamped boat. But James's sister told him that the boat had sunk, and I wondered how she knew.

"She had been in touch with the Coast Guard," he said. "They were flying over. I mean they got the exact time she went down. Most of the old fishermen around here still got the coordinates where she went down, 'cause they were draggin' fishin' nets."

Bronko had told me that fishermen caught their nets on the boat somewhere between Block Island and Montauk.

"Hey," I said, looking at James. "I promised you a beer. Is it time?"

We hopped off the tailgate and continued to talk as we walked back to Salas's.

James said, "I had a dream last night that this place wasn't here anymore."

"You did?"

"Yuh. Just last night I had the dream. It was me and my ex-wife Ethyl were standing up there at Salas's, and I was looking down here and there was nothin' here."

"Wow. The day that I came looking for you, I went up to Parascondola's office, and Nickie talked about change. He said the waterfront down here used to be all coal years ago. And he was talking about how the fishermen have changed, how they're not as tough as they used to be, and there was one other thing he was commenting about, but I can't remember. I tell you, the people that I have met ..."

"A lot of good people ..."

"Oh. Bent over backwards to be helpful to me. Everybody. It has been a great, great adventure."

"I was gone for fifteen years. Fifteen years I was gone. I walked up into that fish house, and everyone of 'em in there—'Little James! Little James is here!' They all gathered around. I hadn't seen 'em in years and years. You know. It was like I had never left."

"There's something very, very special about the fishing community," I said as we stepped back into the din of Salas's bar.

Chapter 47
Final Verification

Bronko Viducic's words haunted me. He said he'd taken a hatch and the polished oak table off the boat. Had she been raised, towed in, and repaired? I called Bronko again.

He assured me that *Three Vs* had sunk. "She went down by the stern," he said. "Her sides burned. She's still laying down there. Fishermen have lost nets on her. She's listed on the charts—a wreck south of Montauk in 158 feet of water."

At one time, I had my NOAA chart of Georges Bank hanging on the wall behind the living-room couch. Andy Dolan, a Mansfield friend, noticed the chart and delighted in teaching me how to read it. His marine credentials allowed him to operate a ferry, but he was happy in a small skiff from which he pulled a lobster trap or two. He told stories about schooners that wrecked and what they should have done to avoid disaster. "You know," he said, "if you had the coordinates of where she went down, you could get a boat and go find her—stand right above her. We couldn't dive; it's too deep. But I have camera equipment with three hundred feet of cable. You could see her."

It was an intriguing idea, but I didn't have the coordinates or enough money to fund such a venture. Besides, it was winter, and there was no way I was going to risk being as cold as I imagined I would be.

The next day, I received a response from the Coast Guard to the request I'd made under the Freedom of Information Act for any and all documentation of *Three Vs* sinking. A one-page "Marine Casualty Investigation Report" supplied a case number, casualty date, notation of clear weather, and a limited narrative description (on the report, *narrative* was spelled with one *r*): "F/V THREE V'S ON FIRE. ALL POB SAFELY TRANSFERRED TO ANOTHER VESSEL." The report listed the coordinates: N 40 57.8, W 71 40.0.

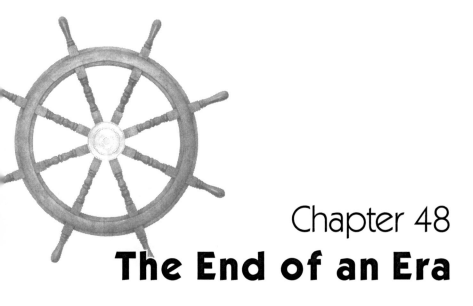

Chapter 48
The End of an Era

My search for *Ellen Marie* gave me far more than I could have imagined: precious relationships, an education about wooden eastern-rig fishing vessels and their fishermen, a love for New Bedford's waterfront and fishing community, and a fondness for South Bristol, Maine. I felt privileged to have tapped into a historic era that had almost passed into oblivion. What a pity, though, that I hadn't appreciated the fishing industry in the 1960s. I'd lived within a half-hour of New Bedford, shopped there before there were malls, yet hadn't paid attention to the major fishing port where fishermen risked their lives to earn an income. I wanted to shout to others, "Do you realize what's been going on in our backyard?"

I had hoped and expected to be able to find *Ellen Marie*, stand on her deck, and experience her reality. The desire was so strong that the psychological defense of denial blocked all suggestions that finding her afloat was unlikely. When Mrs. Wells at the South Bristol Historical Society contacted Nat Hammond to see if he had anything to help with my *Ellen Marie* research, she quoted him as saying, "It's not likely that any of them are still sailing." I secretly resented and then dismissed the discouragement. The skipper of the New Bedford Harbor tour had said he didn't think there were many wooden draggers around. I looked for *Ellen Marie* anyway. I walked the pier twice looking for a boat like *Ellen Marie* that I could tour at the Working Waterfront Festival. Disappointment set in but not the reality that eastern rigs were rare.

Another clue to the passing era was the comment of *Ellen Marie's* fifth owner, Jim Spalt, about the boat's inability to compete. He had upgraded her but still had regarded her as a stepping-stone to a larger steel boat. Donald Calnan, owner number four, suggested the same thing when he referred to the fact that *Ellen Marie* was getting old. Her sale had been a way of improving himself, perhaps by upgrading to a steel vessel.

Captain Woodie Bowers's comments affected my understanding of the wooden eastern-rig era. I remembered his reminiscing about the changes he made in *Ellen Marie* during his seventeen years as captain— replacing an icebox with a refrigerator and putting in hot and cold water. When I told him about touring a steel scalloper, he said, "Those old wood boats compared to boats of today—that's like going from a cave to a castle. Things became so much different when they started building steel boats—the stern trawlers. On the stern trawlers, the whole net goes up on the spool. It's simple. Easy."

I asked him once, "If you wanted the kids today to know something about fishing, what would it be?"

"When they came out with these stern trawlers," he said, "they were so much better—better conditions, less work for the crew—the way the nets come in." Mr. Patenaude, *Ellen Marie's* cook when Woodie Bowers was captain, referred to that too—fewer men and more mechanization.

Another coincidence added to my grasp of the passing of the wooden eastern-rig era. David Andrews asked me to help him track down *Robert C*, a Gamage boat that he had traced to Fairhaven. He was hoping to obtain photographs of the vessel. I located the owner, who told me that *Robert C* was the second boat in at pier 3, so I went to the pier to photograph the vessel myself. If I had been the fisherman who was repeatedly boarding and disembarking the vessel behind *Robert C*, I would have wondered why some woman was taking so much interest in that one vessel. So I explained to the fisherman and included the fact that I had been researching *Ellen Marie*.

"That was my father's boat," he said.

"And who are you?" I asked with surprise. His name was Michael

Calnan, Donald Calnan's son, and he said that I should see *Rianda* at the salvage yard. Learning she was there disturbed me. This was the vessel I had photographed from aboard the *Ocean Princess* a year earlier. He explained how to get to the yard.

I boldly approached the pitiful vessel and took as many photographs as I could before demolition personnel firmly and repeatedly suggested that, given my sandled feet and dangerous material on the ground, it would be in my best interests to leave. Poor *Rianda*. Whatever metal had any value was stripped off her. Her fate after that was a probable sinking, just like the *Angela W* in the federal buyback days of the 1990s. I remembered what Jack Stewardson had written about *Angela W* in the *Standard Times:* "an old wooden dragger with little scrap value." How sad it was now to realize that those words were in the context of the end of an era.

Dave Andrews had sent me a list of Harvey Gamage–built vessels. I searched the Coast Guard's vessel documentation site to see if any of the eastern rigs were still afloat. I found none—at least none afloat with the original names.

Chapter 49
The End

It was a beautiful day—warm for April 14. I parked in front of the Candleworks Restaurant and went to the second floor of the building to pick up tax filings at the Hodgson Pratt office. I was surprised to see my friend John standing at a file cabinet just inside the entrance to his accounting firm when his office was on the floor above and even more surprised by his greeting.

"Rachel! Is this a good day for a walk?"

"Sure," I said. "You have time? I just came to pick up the 1041 and Form 2."

I guessed that he needed a break from preparing tax returns or he'd finished the returns he had to do. We walked through the office and up the stairs to the third floor. John located my returns among several in his office, put on a jacket, and carried the large, thick white envelope of tax reports under his arm to the elevator.

"Where do you want to walk?" I asked. I would have been willing to walk in any direction but wanted most to go to the fish pier.

"Your call," he said. I took the tax package from him to put on the front seat of my car and suggested that we walk over the footbridge to the boats. We trudged the up-and-around stairs to the span across Route 18 and descended, emerging onto pier 3 in front of the red brick visitors center. Thinking that he should see the portrait of Captain Bowers and *Ellen Marie*'s column on the auction board, I asked him if he'd been inside. "With you, as a matter of fact," he said. I wished I remembered but dismissed my inability by focusing on the stern trawlers along the south side of the pier. We walked slowly along, nearly to the pier's end, where a crew had laid out a scallop dredge and was in the process of repairing the chain bag. I was as pleased as if I had recognized an old friend.

"See the guy standing up with the long-handled tool? That tool is a squeezer," I explained to John. "They use cutters and squeezers to repair the chain bags." The man who held the tool looked at us and nodded, perhaps in response to a private conversation, but I enjoyed thinking that he affirmed what I had said. "Before, in the days of *Ellen Marie*," I continued, "they used hammers and tweezers and slammed 'em."

I had learned much about *Ellen Marie*. My primary goal was accomplished. I knew where she was, even though it was impossible to stand on her deck. Walking back across the footbridge, John said, "Well, it seems your *Ellen Marie* adventure has come full circle." More than two years prior, John and I had walked from the Candleworks building to the Moniz Gallery, where I showed him *The Pilot House*. Our walk back to the Candleworks building from pier 3 now seemed to be a fitting end. But it wasn't an end—a hiatus, perhaps. As my research had continually proven, there were still people to meet who had known *Ellen Marie*. There were more related lessons to learn not just about *Ellen Marie* but also about the bigger fishing-industry story of which she was one small, fascinating part.

CPSIA information can be obtained at www.ICGtesting.com
Printed in the USA
BVOW07s0424150914

366712BV00001B/12/P